University of Massachusetts

Amherst, Massachusetts

Written by Seth N. Pouliot
Edited by Kevin Nash

Additional contributions by Omid Gohari, Christina Koshzow,
Chris Mason, Joey Rahimi, Jon Skindzier, Luke Skurman,
Tim Williams, Amanda Ansell, and Kimberly Moore

ISBN # 1-59568-161-1
ISSN # 1552-1389

Special thanks to Babs Carryer, Andy Hannah, LaunchCyte, Tim O'Brien, Bob Sehlinger, Thomas Emerson, Milton Cofield, Andrew Skurman, Barbara Skurman, Bert Mann, Dave Lehman, Daniel Fayock, Chris Babyak, and The Donald H. Jones Center for Entrepreneurship, Terry Slease, Jerry McGinnis, Bill Ecenberger, Idie McGinty, Kyle Russell, Jacque Zaremba, Larry Winderbaum, Paul Kelly, Roland Allen, Jon Reider, Team Evankovich, Julie Fenstermaker, Lauren Varacalli, Abu Noaman, Jason Putorti, Mark Exler, Daniel Steinmeyer, Jared Cohon, Gabriela Oates, Tri Ad Litho.

Bounce Back Team: Molly Lyon, Lindsay Kerwood and Kerri Landers

College Prowler™
5001 Baum Blvd.
Suite 456
Pittsburgh, PA 15213

Phone: (412) 697-1390, 1(800) 290-2682
Fax: (412) 697-1396, 1(800) 772-4972
E-mail: info@collegeprowler.com
Website: www.collegeprowler.com

Welcome to College Prowler™

During the writing of College Prowler's guidebooks, we felt it was critical that our content was unbiased and unaffiliated with any college or university. We think it's important that our readers get honest information and a realistic impression of the student opinions on any campus — that's why if any aspect of a particular school is terrible, we (unlike a campus brochure) intend to publish it. While we do keep an eye out for the occasional extremist — the cheerleader or the cynic — we take pride in letting the students tell it like it is. We strive to create a book that's as representative as possible of each particular campus. Our books cover both the good and the bad, and whether the survey responses point to recurring trends or a variation in opinion, these sentiments are directly and proportionally expressed through our guides.

College Prowler guidebooks are in the hands of students throughout the entire process of their creation. Because you can't make student-written guides without the students, we have students at each campus who help write, randomly survey their peers, edit, layout, and perform accuracy checks on every book that we publish. From the very beginning, student writers gather the most up-to-date stats, facts, and inside information on their colleges. They fill each section with student quotes and summarize the findings in editorial reviews. In addition, each school receives a collection of letter grades (A through F) that reflect student opinion and help to represent contentment, prominence, or satisfaction for each of our 20 specific categories. Just as in grade school, the higher the mark the more content, more prominent, or more satisfied the students are with the particular category.

Once a book is written, additional students serve as editors and check for accuracy even more extensively. Our bounce-back team — a group of randomly selected students who have no involvement with the project — are asked to read over the material in order to help ensure that the book accurately expresses every aspect of the university and its students. This same process is applied to the 200-plus schools College Prowler currently covers. Each book is the result of endless student contributions, hundreds of pages of research and writing, and countless hours of hard work. All of this has led to the creation of a student information network that stretches across the nation to every school that we cover. It's no easy accomplishment, but it's the reason that our guides are such a great resource.

When reading our books and looking at our grades, keep in mind that every college is different and that the students who make up each school are not uniform — as a result, it is important to assess schools on a case-by-case basis. Because it's impossible to summarize an entire school with a single number or description, each book provides a dialogue, not a decision, that's made up of 20 different topics and hundreds of student quotes. In the end, we hope that this guide will serve as a valuable tool in your college selection process. Enjoy!

OMID GOHARI ◯ CHRISTINA KOSHZOW ◯ CHRIS MASON ◯ JOEY RAHIMI ◯ LUKE SKURMAN ◯
Founders of College Prowler™

Table of Contents

Introduction from the Author

At this point, four years is probably close to twenty percent of your life, so you can imagine how important college will be. Just because everyone in the world appears to go to UMass doesn't mean UMass is for everyone in the world. And like everything, the University of Massachusetts in Amherst is undergoing significant changes, not the least of which are financial. So, if I have done my job, the way these changes may potentially shape the experiences people have of this particular school will be expressed in the following pages.

With that said, "The Zoo", a.k.a. UMass, is a great school in a lot of respects. Because of the variety in people, subjects, and ideas you will find here, UMass epitomizes the world you live in and the people you'll work with upon graduation. Keep in mind that Amherst is a college town, and this is conducive to world-class parties, so don't say I didn't warn you. However, out of all the advantages over other schools UMass has to offer, the one that pertained most to me was the level of assistance UMass has for those classified as being "undecided majors". Through an extensive array of general education requirements, first year students get exposed to hundreds of subjects and different ways of thinking.

There is no single "UMass culture". Each residential living area and off-campus apartment complex has a different theme that you will soon become aware of and eventually prefer. Therefore, being open minded at UMass is essential in avoiding the feeling of being overwhelmed. Certain academic departments here are strong and nationally acclaimed, and certain academic departments here are not. This will also become apparent as you read through this.

One thing about UMass you can be sure of is that you won't be the same person when you graduate that you were when you got there, for better or worse. UMass is an exciting place, and more importantly, it is not your parents' house! So, don't focus too heavily on the many easily avoidable negative aspects of UMass, and always remember that you are also there to have fun.

Seth Pouliot, Author
University of Massachusetts

By the Numbers

General Information

University of Massachusetts
Amherst, MA 01003

Control:
Public

Academic Calendar:
Semester

Religious Affiliation:
None

Founded:
1863

Website:
http://www.umass.edu

Main Phone:
(413) 545-0111

Admissions Phone:
(413) 545-0222

Student Body

**Full-Time
Undergraduates:**
17,379

**Part-Time
Undergraduates:**
1,339

**Full-Time Male
Undergraduates:**
9,266

**Full-Time Female
Undergraduates:**
9,452

Female to Male Ratio:
51% to 49%

Admissions

Overall Acceptance Rate:
82%

**Early Decision
Acceptance Rate:**
N/A

Regular Acceptance Rate:
82%

Total Applicants:
16,427

Total Acceptances:
13,461

Freshman Enrollment:
4,077

**Yield (% of admitted
students who actually enroll):**
30%

Early Decision Available?
No

Early Action Available?
No

Regular Decision Deadline:
Feb 1

Must-Reply-By Date:
n/a

**Common Application
Accepted?**
Yes

Supplemental Forms?
Yes

Admissions Phone:
(413) 545-0222

Admissions Website:
http://www.umass.edu/
umhome/admissions/index.html

SAT I or ACT Required?
Either, must be submitted by
February 1st

**SAT I Range
(25th – 75th Percentile):**
1030-1240

**SAT I Verbal Range
(25th – 75th Percentile):**
520-630

**SAT I Math Range
(25th – 75th Percentile):**
510-610

Retention Rate:
82% for freshmen

**Top 10% of
High School Class:**
16%

Application Fee:
$40

**Transfer Applications
Received:**
3,309

**Transfer Apllications
Accepted:**
1,914

Transfer Students Enrolled:
1,153

**Transfer Applicant
Acceptance Rate:**
58%

➜

Financial Information

Tuition in-state:
$9,008

Tuition out-state:
$17,861

Room and Board:
$6,189

Books and Supplies:
$500

**Average Need-Based
Financial Aid Package:**
$9,101
(including loans, work-study,
grants, and other sources)

**Students Who
Applied For Financial Aid:**
59%

Students Who Received Aid:
40%

Financial Aid Forms Deadline:
Febuary 15th (F.A.F.S.A.), May
1st

Financial Aid Phone:
(413) 545-0801

Financial Aid Website:
http://www.umass.edu/umfa

Academics

The Lowdown On...
Academics

Degrees Awarded:
Associate's
Bachelor's
Master's
Doctorate

Most Popular Areas of Study:
19% Social Sciences
14% Business, Management, Marketing
9% Communications, Journalism
7% Psychology
5% Engineering

Full-Time Faculty:
1,218

Faculty with Terminal Degree:
94%

Student-to-Faculty Ratio:
18:1

Average Course Load:
5 courses

→

Undergraduate Schools:

Commonwealth College Honors Program

School of Education

College of Engineering

Graduate School

College of Humanities and Fine Arts

College of Natural Resources and the Environment

College of Natural Sciences and Mathematics

School of Nursing

Isenberg School of Management

School of Public Health and Health Sciences

College of Social and Behavioral Sciences

4 Year Graduation Rate:
44%

5 Year Graduation Rate:
61%

6 Year Graduation Rate:
64%

AP Test Score Requirements
Possible credit for scores of 3 or higher.

IB Test Score Requirements:
Not looked at for admissions purposes, only placement.

Sample Academic Clubs:

Alchemists Anonymous, ALANA Nursing Association, Alpha Lambda Delta, Art History Club, Boltwood Project, Chamber Choir, Debate Team, Environmental Horticultural Club,Hotel Managers, Institute of Industrial Engineers, International, Relations Club, Investment Club, Macintosh Users Group, National Society of Black Engineers, National Society of Collegiate Scholars, NSSLHA, Philosophical Society, Pre-Vet and Animal Science Club, Society of Hispanic Professional Engineers, Society of Physics Students, Society of Women Engineers

Special Degree Options

Graduate Degrees:

MBA Professional Program

The Master of Science in Accounting (MSA) Degree Program

MBA for Professionals

Professional education for Engineering and Applied Science

Master of Science Degree in Plant and Soil Sciences

Master of Music in Music Education

Master's in Public Policy and Administration

Master of Science in Labor Studies

Master of education: 180 Days in Springfield Project

Master of Education/ CAGS: Integrated Day Off-Campus Program

Master of Education: The Collaborative Teacher Education Program

Master of education for Science Teachers

Postbaccalaureate Teacher Licensure

Summer/Fall Licensure Option in Secondary Science and Mathematics

Professional Development Courses for Teachers/Educators

Master of Science (Nursing) Community/School Health

Post-Master's Nurse Practitioners Certificate Program

Worcester Campus Master of Public Health

Online Master of Public Health

Postbaccalaureate Pre-Clinical Program in Communication Disorders.

Undergraduate Degrees:

Online B.S. in Hospitality and Tourism Management

Certificate of Business Administration

Certificate of Online Journalism

Bachelor of General Studies (BGS)

Online RN to BS in Nursing Track

Second Bachelor's Degree track

2003 Summer Field School in Archeology

Criminal Justice Certificate-Online

Adult Part-time Bachelor's Degree

UWW's Bachelor's Degree in Human Services-Mental Retardation/Developmental Disabilities.

Noncredit Certificate and Professional Development Programs:

Conservation Law Enforcement Training

Soil Science Certificate Program

Arts extension Service (AES)

The Certificate Program in Find Raising

Family Business Center

Fundamentals of Arts Management Online

Real Estate Program (REA 100)

Preparation Workshops for the Massachusetts Test for Educator Licensure (MTEL).

Did You Know?

UMass alumni are high achievers. They count among their ranks an astronaut, a Nobel Prize winner, Pulitzer Prize winners, four MacArthur "Genius" award recipients, state and federal lawmakers, Olympic athletes, several Fortune 500 CEOs, and scores of influential scholars, scientists, and engineers.

Students Speak Out On...
Academics

"The teachers at my school are unbelievable! They're willing to help you no matter what, and they always strive to make their classes enjoyable. The general education professors I've had have been decent for the most part, and many of the University's faculty have won awards for their teaching and research."

Q **"I find the teachers to be really accessible.** They all have office hours and encourage students to come talk to them in person if they have questions about the coursework."

Q "Professors at UMass are a mixed bag. **You could get a total idiot** or a complete genius. I personally have lucked out with teachers, but others haven't been so lucky. The teachers within your major are bound to be good, but don't expect too much out of general education courses."

Q "As with any school, the quality of teaching and the professors vary from department to department and person to person. However, UMass seems to have a decent faculty. Almost all of the professors on campus have PhDs. I am in the engineering department and **my teachers are great!**"

Q "One important thing to consider before you go to UMass is the registration process. **Before this year, getting into the classes you wanted was not a problem.** However, this year and probably for a couple of years to come, registering will be very difficult for people because some teachers were cut and the classes fill up very quickly."

Q "**The most respected majors** at UMass are engineering, computer science, psychology, communication, and anything in the school of management."

Q "**It's hard to generalize about the faculty** at UMass. Some of them are amazing and really care about the students. On the other hand, I've had some really terrible professors who are obviously only at the University for research. A lot of introductory classes have more than 400 students, but there are usually small discussion sections with a graduate TA. I've never had a TA who wasn't really helpful."

Q "I've found a lot of the faculty members here to be very liberal. Rarely will you have a teacher without personality or someone who adds his or her own special flair to the course. **All the professors are friendly and willing to help**, but you have to seek them out yourself."

Q "My experience has been that **professors tend to be condescending**. I don't know if that is especially the case at UMass, but I have had a lot of teachers whose egos get in the way of their teaching."

Q "People always talk about how important it is to have a diverse student body, which is true, but I also think **it is important to have a diverse faculty**, and UMass does. The whole point is to get as many points of view as possible."

The College Prowler Take On...
Academics

Many of the students feel as though the faculty at UMass are more than capable of doing their jobs. The most popular and nationally acclaimed departments at UMass are The School of Business, Psychology, Communications, Engineering, and Computer Science. Despite the overwhelmingly large general education courses that each student must satisfy, the breadth and scope of these courses are such that students who have not yet picked a major get exposed to fields that they otherwise would not have considered. Conversely, due to UMass's size, students are sure to experience varying degrees of quality among the faculty.

UMass teachers are very good at making themselves available and ensuring that students are able to get help frequently and on an individual basis. Whether through email, office hours, or weekly tutoring sessions, students can readily access teachers at any point in the semester if they are falling behind. Teacher evaluations conducted at the end of each semester by the students are taken quite seriously by the faculty, keeping the class formats up-to-date and of a high quality. About ninety-nine percent of the larger classes that have 100 students or more also have at least one teaching assistant at the students' disposal. However, depending on the department, many of the TAs do not speak English very well. This is only a problem if your class requires you to take a lab/discussion led by a TA, in which case you can simply switch to another lab/discussion, schedule permitting. One strength that UMass possesses over most other schools is the Five-college Interchange. This program allows students to take courses at any one of the four colleges in the immediate area for no additional charge. These colleges include; Hampshire, Holyoke, Smith, and Amherst.

The College Prowler™ Grade on
Academics: B

A high Academics grade generally indicates that professors are knowledgeable, accessible, and genuinely interested in their students' welfare. Other determining factors include class size, how well professors communicate, and whether or not classes are engaging.

Local Atmosphere

The Lowdown On...
Local Atmosphere

Region:
New England

City, State:
Amherst, MA

Setting:
Suburban

Distance from New York:
3 hours

Distance from Boston:
2 hours

Points of Interest:
Downtown Amherst and Northampton

Closest Movie Theatres:

Amherst Cinema
30 Amity Street
Amherst, Ma 01002
(413) 253-5426

Cinemark
367 Russell Street
Hadley, Ma 01035
(413) 587-4233

Tower Theatres
19 College Street
South Hadley, Ma 01075
(413) 532-3456

Closest Shopping Malls:

Hadley Mall (10 minutes)
Holyoke Mall (25 minutes)

Major Sports Teams:

None, go to Boston!

City Websites

www.amherstcommon.com
www.amherstarea.com

Did You Know?

One way to tell a local from an outsider in Amherst is the way they pronounce Amherst. Outsiders say "Am-herst", while locals say "Am-erst".

Five Fun Facts about Amherst:

- **Scooby Doo was created by a UMass alumnus**, and each of the characters represents one of the five colleges (UMass, Amherst, Smith, Holyoke, and Hampshire).

- The town of Amherst was named after Lord Jeffery Amherst, a British Army Officer who **served in three separate wars**; The Austrian Succession, The Seven Years War, and The French and Indian Wars.

- Sylvester Graham, the Amherst native who was known as "The Philosopher of Sawdust Pudding", was **an early advocate of vegetarianism** and the man for whom the Graham Cracker was named.

- In 1885 Charles King had a barber shop on the second floor of Cook's Block in Amherst, Ma. He was, however, **known less for cutting hair than for his feat of eating fifty raw eggs in fifteen minutes.** Two hundred people gathered on Main Street as he swallowed the eggs and collected the $30 prize.

- **Many famous authors** including Noah Webster, Emily Dickinson, Robert Frost, Jane Dyer, James Tate, Martin Espada, Joseph Langland, and Madeline Blais are from Amherst.

Students Speak Out On...
Local Atmosphere

"Amherst is a small town with two colleges—UMass and Amherst College. Northampton is about five or six miles down the road. It's a trendy town with a lot of shops, restaurants, and music halls. The Northampton district is lively, while Amherst is more laid back."

Q "**We are in the 'Five College' circuit**, with Amherst College, Mount Holyoke, Smith, and Hampshire Colleges all less than twenty minutes away. UMass offers the 'Five College' interchange option of taking classes at any of the surrounding schools for no additional charge."

Q "**The town is definitely a college town**--it's great. I love it because everyone is friendly and there are five universities in the vicinity, just a bus ride away."

Q "Although very rural, **Amherst is in a convenient location** to get to other areas. Boston, New York City, Hartford, and New Haven are all within just a few hours from Amherst."

Q "The center of Amherst is right outside of UMass's campus, in reasonable walking distance. **It's always hopping**, and there's always something to do. There are shops, a mall, and a movie theater just a bus ride away. I personally enjoy quaint little Amherst. It feels old-fashioned."

Q "**You can definitely tell the locals from the outsiders**, but there is a mutual respect because both groups have to be here…Amherst is lovely."

Q "**In every way, Amherst is a college town**. All the businesses are dependent on the colleges around them, but it's a very nice atmosphere. Down near Smith College is Northampton and the bus goes right there. It's a great town with a lot of history, culture, and some very nice restaurants. Everyone loves the movie theater, where the shows are only five dollars."

Q "Amherst is awesome during the school year, but sucks during the summer—seriously, **it is like a ghost town** or something."

Q "I was born and raised here, and will probably never leave. This whole area is **the most beautiful spot in the world** in the fall with the leaves and everything else, it makes you feel like you are in a movie. The town is cute and has so much history, but I can see why so many people go to different places on the weekends. Although, the food here is great and the people are great, and I have had so many great bosses working for the local businesses."

Q "It's like any place really, **it's all what you make of it**. I didn't want to come here right after high school but I didn't get into any of the Boston schools, not like I could afford them anyways. Amherst grew on me, and now I'm glad that I'm not in a big city."

The College Prowler Take On...
Local Atmosphere

Amherst is a lively college town that exemplifies New England's characteristic atmosphere. For me, the richness and volume of culture in Amherst and nearby Northampton is often what I associate with the word "college". During semesters Amherst gets crowded and takes on the likeness of a metropolis, however, during summer and winter breaks, Amherst could pass for any other rural farming community. The visible relationship between native Amherst residents and businesses and the surrounding schools is only one of the synergistic benefits of going to UMass.

As previously mentioned, five major colleges are in the immediate area, and they include; Holyoke, Amherst College, Hampshire College, Smith College, and of course, The University of Massachusetts. Therefore, during the school year Amherst is an exciting town to be in with a lot to do. The restaurants are great, and the center of town is a short walk or free bus ride from campus. Amherst is a very liberal place, where one does not have to look hard to find a political discussion or rally. The bars are pretty good, but the very few clubs in the area leave a lot to be desired. Between the leaves changing color, the almost weekly town festivals, open mic nights, school concerts, and the thousands of other things to become involved with, if you are bored in Amherst it is your own fault. Amherst is also in a good location geographically with Northampton only ten minutes away, and Holyoke (which has a great mall) is twenty-five minutes away.

The College Prowler™ Grade on

Local Atmosphere: C

A high Local Atmosphere grade indicates that the area surrounding campus is safe and scenic. Other factors include nearby attractions, proximity to other schools, and the town's attitude toward students

Safety & Security

The Lowdown On...
Safety & Security

Number of UMass Police:
350

Emergency Phone:
(413) 545-2121

Safety Services:
Emergency Phones located all across campus (a.k.a. "blue phones" or "call boxes")

Rape Defense Classes (RAD)

walking escorts

campus shuttle

Health Services:
University Health Services (413) 577-7000. Open to all students, located near Franklin Dining Hall. "University Health Services provides comprehensive health care, which includes medical, dental, eye care, mental health, specialty clinics and health education services, to a diverse student population and other plan members, as well as urgent care to the University community."

Health Center Office Hours

Open 24 hours a day during the semester and from 8 a.m. to midnight during summer and winter breaks.

Did You Know?

The most read section of the **UMass Daily Collegian** is the "police log" section, which records any arrests that took place on campus.

The UMass police department commonly **patrols campus by horseback.**

A popular scam at UMass is that at the end of each semester, people, who are not affiliated with the University, go around to each dorm and **pay people cash for their textbooks**, usually about $5.00 per book. This practice is illegal, and you can actually get quite a bit more for your books when you are done with them by bringing them directly to the textbook annex- a lesson learned the hard way.

Students Speak Out On...
Safety & Security

"**Every dorm building has security 'check-ins' on the weekends—you have to have a dorm sticker on your student card or be signed in by someone who lives in the building to get in. On campus there are emergency phone boxes, and UMass police patrol the campus. Overall, I feel safe on campus and in my dorm building.**"

Q "**Be aware of your surroundings** and always walk with someone else at night. The campus is pretty well lit and there are 'call boxes' along the paths. As a nursing major I spent many long nights at the library but made sure that I always walked home with friends."

Q "The security on campus is very good, **as far as I'm concerned**. A couple of years ago there were several cases of rape, but since then security has been tighter than ever!"

Q "Security has been really good the last couple of years, but with the recent budget cuts, **the escort service was eliminated**. The escort service was a van driven by a campus police officer that made stops around campus from 5 p.m. - 3 a.m. It was incredibly reliable, but it's gone, replaced with buses that now run later into the wee hours of the morning."

Q "UMass cut the on-campus escort service **because of budget cuts**, but as long as you are smart about being out late, or anytime, for that matter—you will be fine."

Q "As a school of nearly 25,000 undergraduates, **we have occasional problems**. When the Red Sox or Yankees are in the playoffs, there are often huge gatherings in the Southwest residential area, and the cops are usually called in."

Q "I have never felt unsafe at school. **There are always cops** all over the place."

Q "**Occasionally non-students come onto campus** and cause problems, but there isn't any way to prevent that. The only time I have ever felt nervous was walking around at night, both during the week and on the weekends. Just be aware of your surroundings and lock your dorm room whenever you aren't there and stay in crowded places, unless it's a riot."

Q "**Honestly, security and safety need improvement**. There have been attacks and rapes on-campus just this spring, but they're improving on security. There are a lot of resources to use if you're willing to help yourself."

Q "My freshmen year I heard about these people who were all dressed up and came to a Northeast building telling people to leave for an hour so they could fumigate. Then when the students got back all of their valuable stuff was gone. **What a great idea for a robbery!**"

The College Prowler Take On...
Safety & Security

A strong focus is placed on safety and security both on and off campus at UMass. Colleges in general tend to have very high crime rates, and when theft occurs at UMass it is usually nonviolent and involves microscopes, car stereos, and books. Certain areas of UMass experience more crime than others, a statistic that inevitably coincides with population size. These areas include Southwest, parking lots, and the many off campus apartment complexes. Students can take many steps to protect themselves from crime such as walking with friends, walking in well-lit areas, being vocal, locking doors, never leaving a personal item unattended, carrying a cell phone, and remaining alert at all times.

On the weekends, UMass completely lives up to its nickname "The Zoo". Quite often parties result in riots and fights, which occur not only at campus housing, but also at the off-campus housing. There is a police department located right in the middle of campus, and they do a very good job of keeping things from getting out-of-hand. Also, UMass has an amazing transportation system that is free, and makes it very safe to travel around Amherst at night. Between the Amherst Police Department and the UMass Police Department, most students seem to feel safe on campus.

B

The College Prowler™ Grade on
Safety & Security: B

A high grade in Safety & Security means that students generally feel safe, campus police are visible, blue-light phones and escort services are readily available, and safety precautions are not overly necessary.

Computers

The Lowdown On...
Computers

High-Speed Network?
Yes

Wireless Network?
Yes

Number of Labs:
11

Average Number of Computers:
25

Operating Systems:
2 Mac labs
9 PC labs

24-Hour Labs

Yes, Residential Labs

Charge to Print?

Depends on the lab, library labs have free printing

Services

O.I.T. (Office of Information Technology) charges competitive prices ($30/hour) for the following services:

- Any hardware repair or upgrade
- OS recovery, damaged or missing files
- OS installation (reinstall, clean install, or upgrade)
- Application installation (reinstall, clean install, or upgrade)
- Virus Removal, hard drive or removable media
- Date recovery from failed hard drive
- Data back-up to removable media for archive
- Data transfer (PC to Mac; old to new machines; old to new drives)

Did You Know?

 You must **purchase a $30/semester OIT account** to use any of the labs, or to have internet access in your dorm room

If you have reliable access to a computer with the Internet you can **take many of your courses online** and never change out of your pajamas!

As of last year, all registration for courses, and most other **administrative matters can be handled online** through a program called "SPIRE" on the UMass website (https://spire. umass.edu/saha/index.asp).

Students Speak Out On...
Computers

"There's a bunch of computer labs. I personally have never had a problem getting a computer in one. I have my own computer and it's easier to have one in my room than to make time to go to the library or something, but it's really not a necessity. Every building has Ethernet access, a high-speed Internet connection."

Q "**Definitely bring your own** computer to campus. It is much easier, and some classes send you email or require you to do some homework on the Web."

Q "The computer network is generally awesome. Each room has two Ethernet ports, so **you and your roommate can each have your own account**. Some computer labs are busy, while others aren't at all. If you can bring at least a laptop with an Ethernet card, you'll be golden, because you can do nearly anything from your room."

Q "**Computer labs are rarely crowded**, unless there is a class using the computers. There are always some computers available in the library."

Q "Almost everyone has their own computer—**I don't know anyone without one**."

Q "**The dorm Internet connections are great**—two LAN connections in each room! Two dorms on campus have computer labs, as well as the Research Center and the library. They're usually pretty empty."

Q "I work in the computer labs on campus, and **I promise they're never too busy**, except during finals. There are many labs on campus with both Macs and PCs."

Q "Setting up my computer account for the computer in my room was the biggest headache, except that I didn't even have a choice because most of my classes required us to do homework on the internet. **The computer labs in the library offer free printing**, but sometimes they are so busy, not to mention the hike it takes just to get from my room to the library. The internet is fast around here; on the other hand, the computers in the dormitory labs are extremely old and outdated. One good thing about living in the dorms though is that you always know someone with a computer, and usually a printer. Even with all this said, I recommend any new students to bring their own."

Q "The purpose of **technology is to make life easier**, but not at UMass."

Q "Considering how old some of the buildings are at UMass, the internet hook-ups are pretty decent. The library computers are useful, but you have to figure out when there will be classes held at them so you can avoid that. **I never really had any major problems** concerning the computers here."

The College Prowler Take On...
Computers

Ironically, UMass has a very reputable Computer Science program yet disappointing resources for everyone else. Relying on campus computer labs is risky because they have bizarre hours and get extremely packed. On the bright side, UMass does have excellent Internet access called Ethernet. Getting a mandatory O.I.T. account is relatively easy, and cheap, but if anything goes wrong it can take days before you actually get to speak with a live customer service representative. The Office of Information Technologies is wretchedly understaffed, a problem that is only compounded at the beginning of each semester when all the students are trying to get squared away at the same time.

The library labs probably have the nicest computers, and free printing, which is huge. Regardless of whether you are going to live on or off campus, bring your own computer. If you don't have one, and can't afford to purchase a new one, just sell your car because you won't need that.

The College Prowler™ Grade on

Computers: C+

A high grade in Computers designates that computer labs are available, the computer network is easily accessible, and the campus' computing technology is up-to-date.

Facilities

The Lowdown On...
Facilities

Campus Size:
1,463 Acres

Athletic Center:
William D. Mullins Center
Boyden Gymnasium
Totman Gymnasium

Student Center:
Lincoln Campus Center

Libraries:
W.E.B. Dubois Library (the big one you can see from outer space)
Biological Sciences Library (Morrill Science Center)
Physical Sciences and Engineering Library (Lederle)
AIMS Film/Video Library (The Photo Center Building)

➔

Popular Places to Chill:
Campus Pond
Dorms
Student Union and Campus
Center
Amherst Center
Dining commons.

What Is There to Do On Campus?
The Bluewall in the University Center often has live music perform along with open mic nights. Most of the dorms have pool tables and lounges with nice TVs where you can watch movies or just relax. Also, The Stockbridge building and The Fine Arts Center both have frequently occurring plays throughout the year that are quite popular.

Movie Theatre on Campus?
No

Bowling on Campus?
No

Bar on Campus?
Yes. Bluewall, The University Center

Coffeehouse on Campus?
Yes. Bluewall coffee house, The University Center

Favorite Things to do?
Intramural sports, Party, join one of the over 200 Registered Student Organizations, go on a hike, go to the Holyoke mall.

Students Speak Out On...
Facilities

> "The facilities are okay—some departments are better than others, but they're all decent."

Q "The athletics department and the computer labs **definitely get hooked up with cool stuff**. The student union isn't bad, but it could use some work."

Q "**There are lots of computer labs around campus,** in places like the English building and the library. The student union and the campus center usually offer a lot going on."

Q "The athletic facilities could be better, but the **student center has a lot of stuff in it** and people always hang out there."

Q "**The gym has really crowded weight lifting rooms**, but it's good for basketball and aerobic exercise."

Q "I really like the campus center, where there is a big store, **a bunch of places to eat**, lots of different clubs to join, and places to study. The library is huge—it's over twenty stories high."

Q "The athletic facilities are very close to the Southwest residential area, and because sports are so huge here, **the facilities are very well kept**."

Q "The facilities are very cool! **The campus center is always hopping** with something. Everything is really right there at your fingertips, and there is so much!"

Q "The campus center and student union are **right in the middle of campus** and offer many different things like dining areas, crafts centers, a campus store, and campus tables to advertise the different registered student organizations."

Q "**Computer labs are located in four areas**. They are all pretty nice and updated, and there's one located within five minutes of each residence area."

Q "We have **a nice stadium and two good gyms**. There are also fitness centers in various residence halls on campus."

Q "**The facilities on campus are kind of a mixed bag**: there are some old-fashioned, typical New England-style buildings and there are some hideous, modern, concrete buildings."

Q "This year **the campus was really ugly** because of all the construction going on in front of the Fine Arts Center. It really depends, UMass has a lot of facilities. The Mullins Center is great, and there is always something happening there. But the gyms for the students are awful, and you'll be lucky if you don't have to stand in line for a treadmill. If you want to see what the nicer UMass facilities are, just take a look at the brochure!"

Q "I've had classrooms where I'd rather sit on the floor than in the chairs, and I've had classrooms where it was hard to stay awake because the chairs are so damn comfortable. They just put an addition on Isenberg and **I've never seen such beautiful, technologically advanced classrooms**."

The College Prowler Take On...
Facilities

To a new student, the sheer number and range of facilities at UMass is impressive and a little intimidating. Overall, the general feeling is that UMass facilities are maintained well and offer us students everything we need and most of what we want. Many of the buildings could use a facelift as they appear to have been designed by an architect who lived in communist Russia. The W.E.B. Dubois Library is twenty-six stories tall and offers everything you could ever need as a student. Unknown to most students, when the library was designed the engineers forgot to take into account the weight of the books, so every year this massive building sinks one inch further into the ground. With some exceptions, the buildings on campus are not very architecturally pleasing, but they certainly possess a lot of history and character. There are only two gyms on campus for students to go lift weights and do cardio exercises for free, but both are tiny and have outdated equipment.

The pulse of UMass is located at the campus center, where vendors and student organizations compete against each other for your precious attention. This complex, which includes the Student Union, accommodates everything from cafeterias to a mini Wal-Mart known as The University Store. This building also contains a long heavily traversed tunnel where so many flyers are posted that you can barely see the wall behind it. Each facility on campus has its own disposition and usually looks completely different from every other facility. My advice to anyone contemplating enrollment at UMass, whose decision rests solely on the condition of its facilities, is to deliberate as to whether or not the building housing their major is one they can tolerate spending a lot of time in.

B-

The College Prowler™ Grade on

Facilities: B-

A high Facilities grade indicates that the campus is aesthetically pleasing and well-maintained; facilities are state-of-the-art, and libraries are exceptional. Other determining factors include the quality of both athletic and student centers and an abundance of things to do on campus.

Campus Dining

The Lowdown On...
Campus Dining

Freshman Meal Plan Requirement?

Yes

Meal Plan Average Cost:

Three options; Basic ($1,206.50 per semester), Value ($1,256.50 per semester), Deluxe ($1,288 per semester)

24-Hour On-Campus Eating?

No

Places to Grab a Bite with Your Meal Plan

Blue Wall

Location: Campus Center
Food: Morning stuff
Favorite Dish: Bagel with cream cheese
Hours: Sun-Thurs 7:30 a.m.-11 p.m.

Hatch Food Court

Location: Campus Center,
Food: Italian, Mexican, American
Favorite Dish: Taco salad
Hours: Mon-Fri, 11 a.m.-2 p.m.

→

Starbucks Coffee Cart
Location: Campus Center
Food: I'll give you one guess
Favorite dish: Either the coffee or the coffee
Hours: Mon-Fri, 6:30 a.m.-3 p.m.

Douglass Dining Center
Location: Douglass
Food: Wraps, quesadillas, "home-cooked" food, soups
Favorite dish: Chicken and cheese quesadilla
Hours: Mon- Fri 10 a.m.- 8 p.m.

Danforth Dining Center
Location: Susan B. Anthony
Food: All buffet style, all-you-can-eat, varying foods
Favorite dish: Chinese stir-fry
Hours: Mon- Fri. 4:30 p.m.-8 p.m., Sat., Sun. 9:00- 2 p.m., 4:30 p.m.-8 p.m.

Hillside Café
Location: Susan B. Anthony
Food: Pizza, desserts, sandwiches, coffee drinks, smoothies
Favorite Food: Strawberry yogurt smoothie
Hours: Mon. – Sun. 12 p.m. – 1 a.m., Closed, Mon- Fri 4:30- 8:30

The Meliora
Location: Above Douglass Dining Center
Food: Sit-down with sandwiches, soup. entrees, desserts
Favorite food: Grilled cheese
Hours: Mon-Fri. 11:30 a.m.- 2 p.m.

The MarketPlace Café
Location: Campus Center
Food: American, Asian
Favorite Dish: General Tso Chicken
Hours: Mon-Fri 8 a.m.-3 p.m.

4 Residential dining Halls:
Franklin, Berkshire, Hampshire, and Worcester
Location: Near the dorms
Food: everything
Favorite Dish: Pizza
Hours: Mon-Sun 7 a.m.-2 a.m.

Places on Campus to Eat Without a Meal Plan:

Earthfoods
Location: Student Union
Food: A Vegetarian Collective
Favorite Dish: Humus Wrap
Hours: 11 a.m.-3 p.m. Monday-Friday

Greenough Sub Shop

Location: Greenough Basement, Central Residential Area

Food: Subs (aka "grinders")

Favorite Dish: Cheeseburger Sub

Hours: Sun-Thursday 4 p.m.-midnight, Sat 6 p.m.-midnight

Sylvan Snack Bar

Location: McNamara Basement, Sylvan Residential Area

Food: Subs, ice cream, bagels, burritos

Favorite Dish: Frozen Yogurt

Hours: Sun-Thurs 7 p.m.-1 a.m., Fri-Sat 9 p.m.-2 a.m. (They Deliver!)

Newman Center Cafeteria

Location: Newman Center

Food: American

Favorite Dish: Chicken Caesar Wrap

Hours: 7 a.m.-7 p.m.

People's Market

Location: Student Union

Food: Hippy

Favorite Dish: Indonesian Wrap

Hours: Mon & Fri 8:45 a.m.-4 p.m., Tues-Thurs 8:45 a.m.-5 p.m.

Other Options:

Students can utilize the "Grab and Go" at three different places on campus for the price of one meal. This alternative offers you a sandwich, snack/piece of fruit, and drink, and is great for when you are in a hurry. The three places where you can do this are; The Worcester C-store, and The Berkshire and Hampshire Dining Commons.

Student Favorites:

People's Market

Bluewall

Did You Know?

It is **cheaper to get an off-campus apartment and buy groceries** than it is to pay for room and board. As a freshmen and a sophomore, you must live in the dorms and get a meal plan unless you live within a forty-mile radius of UMass and commute… hint hint.

Students Speak Out On...
Campus Dining

"There are several good places to eat on campus. The most popular place is the Blue Wall and Coffee Shop. The student union has The People's Market—a great place to grab coffee, juice, and bagels."

Q "**I found the dining commons to be fine** my first two years at UMass—I ate at the Franklin dining hall, but by junior year I was sick of it and just bought food for my room."

Q "Campus dining commons, called DCs, aren't so hot. **The best DCs are in the Southwest living area**, but you don't have to live in Southwest to eat there."

Q "Personally, I think the DCs are pretty good—**I've had worse**. When I eat on campus I go for Hampshire or Berkshire. Berkshire has the greatest stir fry. You can get something to eat at the Blue Wall or at People's Market, too—both are great places."

Q "I'll be honest—the dining commons food sucks. It's mandatory to eat there for your first two years, which is a huge pain in the butt. **We have a few good places on-campus**, though. The Hatch, Bluewall, and Greenough Sub Shop are the most common favorites. They serve things ranging from soups and salads to pizza and subs. Your campus meal plan swipes you into these places. The Hatch is the best place to eat on campus, though few freshmen know this valuable fact."

Q "Most of us eat at the DCs, and the food isn't bad. If you don't like what they have in the hot food line, there are 'usuals' that they offer everyday: the grill, with burgers and fries; a fresh sandwich bar; a salad bar; and fresh fruit. These things are there everyday, without fail. **People say that Worcester is the best** DC on campus. I eat there daily, but only because it's near my residential area, Sylvan."

Q "There are vegetarian meals, vegan meals, and always subs and pizza in the dining commons. **For delivery, there is awesome food!** We have a great calzone place called DP Dough and a place that delivers boneless wings. There's even delivery for cookies and ice cream from a store called Sugar Jones."

Q "The dining halls on campus offer standard campus food. **They're buffet style**, with full salad bars, pasta areas, and deli areas. There are also some other places on campus to eat—the Bluewall in the campus center is good."

Q "Basically, the dining hall food on-campus sucks. Fortunately for us there's a program called 'Off-Campus Meal Plan' (OCMP). You can pay extra money to put food from off-campus restaurants on a special card they issue. **It's kind of expensive**, but it's definitely worth it. A couple of good places to eat on-campus are not included in the basic meal plan—the Hatch in the basement of the student union is a good one."

Q "**There are three places on campus** where you can do a Grab-and-Go; The Worcester C-Store, and the Berkshire and Hampshire dining commons. I don't remember if you can use your meal plan, but it is very convenient."

The College Prowler Take On...
Campus Dining

UMass dining commons are nothing special. Although, considering the number of people they feed everyday, Food Services keeps the shelves stocked and the cafeterias relatively clean. They have foods for breakfast, lunch, and dinner that are cooked everyday like pizza, pasta, and salad, and entrees that change every day. If you want a little variety, your best bet is to eat at one of the many cafeterias located all across campus. In my opinion, the best two are The Newman Center and The Hatch where you can find anything from Mexican to Asian at a reasonable price. Students have the option of purchasing off-campus meal plans (OCMP), allowing them to dine at many of the restaurants located near campus.

If, at the end of the semester, you haven't fully redeemed all the meals you purchased you don't get back the remaining balance. Therefore, buying the most basic and inexpensive meal plan is highly advisable until you figure it out for yourself; I promise you won't starve at UMass - if anything, you will gain weight. Saying that one dining common is better than another really depends on what type of food you like, because each one is better at making one of the regular dishes than the rest of them. Over half of the non-dormitory buildings have someplace to eat, even if it's just a small coffee and pastry stand. And if you are a coffee drinker almost everywhere on campus has good coffee, even the dining commons. Regardless of what you like, and no matter how picky an eater you are, somewhere on campus will have food that you are able to choke down.

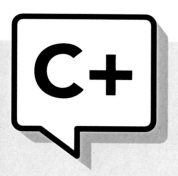

The College Prowler™ Grade on

Campus Dining:
C+

Our grade on Campus Dining addresses the quality of both school-owned dining halls and independent on-campus restaurants as well as the price, availability, and variety of food.

Off-Campus Dining

The Lowdown On...
Off-Campus Dining

Restaurant Prowler:
Popular Places to Eat!

Amber Waves
Food: Thai
Address: 55 University Drive
Phone: (413) 549-9464
Cool Features: Beautiful Paintings by local artists on the walls (usually for sale)
Price: $8.00 and under per person

Amherst Brewing Company
Food: American and Beer, the 5th food group
Address: 63 Main Street
Phone: (413) 253-4400
Fax: (413) 253-4022
Cool Features: Great place to chill on the weekends, live music
Price: $12.00 and under per person
Hours: Everyday 11:30 a.m.-1 a.m.

➜

Antonio's

Food: Pizza

Address: 31 North Pleasant Street

Phone: (413) 253-0808

Fax: (413) 253-8951

Cool Features: Always crowded, you have to see it to believe it

Price: $2.50/slice...worth every penny

Hours: Everyday 10 a.m.-1 a.m.

Banana Rama

Food: Smoothies

Address: 33 North Pleasant Street

Cool Features: free supplements

Price: $4.00-5.00 per smoothie

Black Sheep Deli and Bakery

Food: Gourmet Sandwiches

Address: 79 Main Street

Phone: (413) 253-3442

Fax: (413) 253-6544

Cool Features: Friendly people, great atmosphere, good music (live bands on Sunday)

Price: $5.50 and under per person

Hours: Mon-Thurs 7 a.m.-9 p.m., Fri & Sat 7 a.m.-10 p.m.

Special note: I used to work here, I highly recommend the Black Sheep Beget

Bueno Y Sano

Food: Burritos

Address: 46 Main Street

Phone: (413) 253-4000

Cool Features: Enormous burritos

Price: $5.00-7.00 per burrito

Hours: Everyday 11 a.m.-9 p.m.

China Inn

Food: Chinese

Address: 11 North Pleasant Street

Phone: (413) 253-8868

Cool Features:

Hours: Mon-Sat 11:30 a.m.-10 p.m.

DP Dough

Food: Calzones

Address: 96 North Pleasant Street

Phone: (413) 256-1616... memorize this number now!

Cool Features: They deliver

Price: $5.50 per calzone

Hours: Tues-Sun 4 p.m.-2 a.m.

Judie's

Food: Mostly American

Address: 51 North Pleasant Street

Phone: (413) 253-3491

Cool Features: Good View of Main Street while you eat

Price: $8.00-10.00 per person

Hours: Tues-Sun 11:30 a.m.-10 p.m., close at 11 p.m. on Fri & Sat

La Veracruzana

Food: Mexican

Address: 63 South
Pleasant Street

Phone: (413) 253-6100

Cool Features: Yucca (fried
cactus, tastes better than it
sounds), imported Mexican
beer

Price: $8.00 and under
per person

Panda East

Food: Fried Panda and Dolphin
Burgers served on endangered
baby-seal buns

Address: 103 North
Pleasant Street

Phone: (413) 256-8923

Cool Features: Great
Chinese food

Price: $10.00 and under
per person

Hours: Mon-Thurs
11 a.m.-10 p.m.,
Fri & Sat 11 a.m.-11 p.m.

Paradise of India

Food: Indian

Address: 87 Main Street

Phone: (413) 256-1067

Cool Features: Take out

Price: $15.00 per person

Hours: Everyday
11:30 a.m.-2:30 p.m.
& 4:30 p.m.-9:30 p.m.

Pasta E Basta

Food: Italian

Address: 26 Main Street

Phone: (413) 256-3550

Cool Features: Great food
that you watch them make

Price: $8.00 per person

Hours: Mon-Thurs
11 a.m.-9 p.m.,
Fri & Sat close at 9:30 p.m.

The Pub

Food: American

Address: 15 East
Pleasant Street

Phone: (413) 549-1200

Cool Features: Turns into
a club at night

Price: $12.00-15.00
per person

Hours: Mon-Thurs
11:30 a.m.-9:30 p.m.,
Sundays open at 11 a.m.,
weekends close at 1 a.m.

Wings

Food: Chicken

Address: 55 University Drive

Phone: (413) 549-9464

Cool Features: Best Wings
in town, they deliver

Price: $5.00-10.00 per person

Favorites of Students Living on Campus:
Wings
DP Dough

Favorites of Students Living Off Campus:
Bueno Y Sano
Antonio's

Closest Grocery Store:
Stop and Shop
456 Russell St (RTE 9)
Hadley, Ma
(413) 253-3227

Best Pizza:
Antonio's

Best Chinese:
China Inn

Best Breakfast:
Black Sheep Deli

Best Wings:
Wings

Best Healthy:
Bueno Y Sano
Banana Rama

Best Place to Take Your Parents:
The Pub

Did you know?

As a meal plan option, **you can purchase O.C.M.P. (Off Campus Meal Plan),** which most of these listed restaurants will accept. However, it really only makes sense to get O.C.M.P. if you own a vehicle, or if you don't mind taking the bus all the time.

A company known as Delivery Express (413-549-0077) will **deliver food from any of Amherst's restaurants** to you.

Students Speak Out On...
Off-Campus Dining

> "Amherst and Northampton are great for dining out. There are several restaurants in the area that range in price as well as the types of food they offer."

Q "Downtown, **Antonio's has awesome pizza**, Panda East has great Chinese food, and Applebee's, Chili's, and Friendly's offer reliable favorites on Route 9. Great delivery places like Pinocchio's and Wings bring the off-campus dining experience to those who don't want to wander."

Q "The Amherst-Northampton area has some of the best restaurants ever. **There's a wide variety of different types** of food to eat, including pizza, hamburgers, burritos, Chinese, Thai, Indian, and Italian. It's all very yummy! My personal favorites are Antonio's pizza, Bueno Y Sano for burritos, Amherst Brewing Company, and Bart's Ice Cream."

Q "Restaurants off-campus are all very good. There is Judie's, in the center of Amherst--**very good food, but very expensive**. The center of town is also home to Antonio's, a popular pizza joint, and Amherst Brewing Company, a very good restaurant which I have been to multiple times. It's your typical grill-type restaurant with nightly specials."

Q "Whether you live in the dorms or off campus **you can get everything delivered to you**. And the places in Northampton are worth checking out even though they are farther away. Pinocchio's in Northampton is probably my favorite place to go for pizza even though everyone else says Antonio's."

Q "Restaurants off-campus are **usually really good and fairly cheap**. Since Amherst attracts a lot of people from all over, there is a wide variety of places to eat, from basic pizza places to Thai and Indian. Most of them accept OCMP. There are also a ton of late-night delivery places, delivering basically everything you could ever want. If the place you want doesn't deliver, you can call Delivery Express. They will go to any restaurant in the Amherst area and pick it up for you."

Q "**Antonio's is hands down the best pizza place ever**. They come up with slices you could never imagine on your own. Wings has awesome chicken, and the Sub is the best sub place I've ever eaten at. Amherst Brewing Company is slightly expensive, but it's really good and has live music all the time. Fifteen minutes outside campus is Northampton, a small city with some of the best restaurants in the state, not to mention the 4+ music venues and a great music scene."

Q "Ninety percent of the businesses in Amherst are restaurants, and ninety percent of those have great food, in fact **that is why I came to UMass**."

Q "You can get any type of food here, **no matter what you are in the mood for**. I try to eat at a new restaurant every day because there is so much to choose from. They usually have good music playing in the background too."

The College Prowler Take On...
Off-Campus Dining

The restaurants off campus are amazing, and most of them deliver. You can get good food in Amherst at places like Bueno Y Sano, Veracruzana, Black Sheep Deli, Antonio's, Amber Waves, Pasta Y Basta, and D.P. Dough (the best calzones I've ever had, and yes, they deliver). There are also many good restaurants in neighboring Northampton that are well worth the pilgrimage. Working at one of the off-campus restaurants in Amherst has a lot of fringe benefits, namely, free food! A lot of the restaurants will trade foods among employees, so essentially, when you work at one restaurant, you can also eat for free at the other restaurants in town, but you didn't hear this from me.

Another great part about Amherst restaurants is that they are a fun place to hang out. They are always playing good music, and most have beautiful murals painted all over the walls. On the weekends they stay open very late to cater to the many people walking around town. When I went to UMass as a freshman, I learned which restaurants to eat at in town before I even knew where the dining commons were; I simply cannot say enough about the quality of restaurants in Amherst and Northampton.

The College Prowler™ Grade on
Off-Campus Dining: B+

A high off-campus dining grade implies that off-campus restaurants are affordable, accessible, and worth visiting. Other factors include the variety of cuisine and the availability of alternative options (vegetarian, vegan, Kosher, etc.).

On-Campus Housing

The Lowdown On...
On-Campus Housing

Room Types:
Coed dorms (89%)
Women's dorms (6%)
Men's dorms (1%)
Sorority housing (2%)
Fraternity housing (2%)
Single-student apartments
Married-student apartments
Housing for disabled students
Housing for international students
Other housing

Undergrads on Campus:
59%

Percentages of Students in:
Singles: 7%
Doubles: 81%
Triples/Suites: 12%

Number of Dorms:
41

Number of University-Owned Apartments:
345

→

UMass Dorms:
Dormitory Cluster: Northeast

Overview: "The Northeast residential area is comprised of nine traditionally-styled buildings that form a quadrangle around a large grassy area known as the quad. The residence halls in Northeast are generally smaller than many of the other area halls."

The following 9 dorms are in Northeast:

Crabtree Hall

Profile: Phone, Cable TV, Ethernet, recreation room with pool table, TV room/lounge, Fireplace, Kitchen, Laundry and vending machines

Typical Room Dimensions: 14' by 15' ft, single/bunkable beds

Special Features: Coed, First-Year Engineering

Dwight Hall

Profile: Phone, Cable TV, Ethernet, TV Lounge, Recreation room with pool table, Kitchen, Laundry and vending machines

Typical Room Dimensions: 14' by 15' ft, single/ bunkable or loftable beds

Special Features: Coed, Asian-American Floor

Leach Hall

Profile: Phone, Cable TV, Ethernet, TV Lounge, Recreation room with pool table, Kitchen, Laundry and vending machines, bike room

Typical Room Dimensions: 14' by 15' ft, single/bunkable or loftable beds, bookcases

Special Features: Coed, First-Year Engineering

Lewis Hall

Profile: Phone, Cable TV, Ethernet, Wellness Center, Study lounges on each Floor, Classroom and seminar room, music room with piano, Recreation room with pool table and fireplace, Kitchen, Laundry and vending machines

Typical Room Dimensions: 14' by 15' ft, single/bunkable or loftable beds, bookcases

Special Features: Coed, International House Program, 9-month Residence Hall

Hamlin Hall

Profile: Phone, Cable TV, Ethernet, Recreation room with pool table and ping pong table, Kitchen, Laundry and vending machines

Typical Room Dimensions: 14' by 15' ft, single/bunkable or loftable beds, bookcases

Special Features: All-male residency

Mary Lyon Hall

Profile: Phone, Cable TV, Ethernet, Classroom/seminar room, Lounge with pool table and piano, Kitchen, Laundry and vending machines

Typical Room Dimensions: 14' by 15' ft, single/bunkable beds, bookcases

Special Features: Coed, 1 all female floor, 2 in 20 floor (for gay, lesbian, bisexual, and transgender students)

Johnson Hall

Profile: Phone, Cable TV, Ethernet, Study Lounge, Recreation room with pool table and TV, Kitchen, Laundry and vending machines

Typical Room Dimensions: 14' by 15' ft, single/bunkable beds, bookcases

Special Features: Coed

Thatcher Hall

Profile: Phone, Cable TV, Ethernet, Community study lounges, Recreation room with pool table/TV/fireplace, Computer room, Kitchen, Laundry and vending machines,

Typical Room Dimensions: 14' by 15' ft, single/bunkable or loftable beds, bookcases

Special Features: Coed, Max Kade German Studies Center, Thatcher Foreign Language Program (Chinese, French, German, Italian, Japanese, Spanish)

Knowlton Hall

Profile: Phone, Cable TV, Ethernet, Study lounge, Several kitchens, Recreation room with pool table/TV/fireplace, Laundry and vending machines

Typical Room Dimensions: 14' by 15' ft, single/bunkable beds, bookcases

Special Features: All-female residency, United Asian Learning Resource Center, Barrier-free and accessible for physically disabled students

Dormitory Cluster: Central

Overview: "Close to mid-campus lies The Central Residence Area which is made up of nine traditionally-styled buildings."

The following 9 dorms are in Central:

Baker Hall

Profile: Phone, Cable TV, Ethernet, Lounges on most floors, Kitchen, Basement lounge with pool table and vending machines, Laundry facility, Lounge on first floor with TV

Typical Room Dimensions: 13' by 14' ft, single/bunkable beds, bookcases

Special Features: Coed, 24 hour quiet floor, First year general education program

Brett Hall

Profile: Phone, Cable TV, Ethernet, Lounges on most floors, third floor lounge with kitchen, Basement lounge with kitchen and TV, Quiet study, Laundry facility, Vending machines

Typical Room Dimensions: 13' by 14' ft, single/bunkable beds, bookcases

Special Features: Coed, 9-month residence hall option, Central area resident government offices, fully accessible for physically disabled students

Brooks Hall

Profile: Phone, Cable TV, Ethernet, Lounge on most floors, Kitchen available on first and third floor lounges, Recreation room with pool table and TV

Typical Room Dimensions: 13' by 14' ft, single/ bunkable beds, bookcases

Special Features: Coed, Fully accessible to the physically disabled, Alcohol-free residence, 24-hour quiet hall

Butterfield Hall

Profile: Phone, Cable TV, Ethernet, Community study lounge with fireplace, Kitchen, TV room, Band practice room, Laundry, recreation room with pool table

Typical Room Dimensions: 13' by 14' ft, single/bunkable beds, bookcases

Special Features: Coed

Chadbourne Hall

Profile: Phone, Cable TV, Ethernet, Lounge on first floor with TV, Kitchens on four floors, Recreation room with pool table, Laundry and vending machines

Typical Room Dimensions: 13' by 14' ft, single/bunkable beds, bookcases

Special Features: Coed, Native American Floor, The Josephine White Eagle Native American Cultural center

Gorman Hall

Profile: Phone, Cable TV, Ethernet, Study lounges on most floors, Kitchen on first floor, Oversized community lounge with large screen TV, Laundry and vending machines

Typical Room Dimensions: 13' by 14' ft, single/bunkable or loftable beds, bookcases

Special Features: Coed, NUANCE (a multicultural living community), Wellness floor

Greenough Hall

Profile: Phone, Cable TV, Ethernet, Community study lounge, Kitchen on two floors, Large community lounge with TV, Laundry and vending machines

Typical Room Dimensions: 13' by 14' ft, single/bunkable beds, bookcases

Special features: Coed, Greenough Snack Bar, Wellness floor

Van Meter Hall

Profile: Phone, Cable TV, Ethernet, Large community lounge with TV, Kitchen, Dance studio, large multi-purpose room used for performances/presentations/studying, Vending machines, Two laundry facilities

Typical Room Dimensions: 13' by 14' ft, single/bunkable beds, bookcases

Special Features: Coed, Two Female-only floors

Wheeler Hall

Profile: Phone, Cable TV, Ethernet, Community study lounge, Kitchen with eating area, recreation room with pool table and TV, Central Gallery (managed by the Residential Arts Program featuring art from students and faculty), Laundry and vending machines

Typical Room Dimensions: 13' by 14' ft, single/bunkable beds, bookcases

Special Features: Coed

Dormitory Cluster: Southwest

Overview: "The Southwest Residential Area, the largest on campus, houses 5,400 students in its five high-rise towers, and eleven low-rise residence halls. The area has a distinctly urban flavor, and the community spirit in Southwest is lively and active."

The following 16 dorms are in Southwest:

Coolidge Hall

Profile: High Rise Tower, Phone, Cable TV, Ethernet, Study lounges on each floor, Kitchens on three floors, Classrooms, Club Coolidge (a student-run recreation floor with TV, arcade and table games, and snack foods), Laundry facilities on several floors, vending machines on first floor

Typical Room Dimensions: 13' by 12.75 ft (corner rooms), single/bunkable beds, bookcases

Special Features: Coed, several all-male floors, Z-rooms, Harambee Program for students of African heritage, First year general education program

Crampton Hall

Profile: Low Rise, Phone, Cable TV, Ethernet, lounges/study areas on several floors (some with TV's), Large kitchen with cooking and dining facilities, PC computer lab, laundry and vending machines

Typical Room Dimensions: 12' by 14' ft, single/bunkable or loftable beds, bookcases

Special Features: Coed, Graduate and nontraditionally-aged student housing, 12-month housing option

Emerson

Profile: Low Rise, Phone, Cable TV, Ethernet, Lounges on every floor, Kitchen with Adjacent eating area, Classroom, Laundry and vending machines

Typical Room Features: 12' by 18' ft, single/bunkable beds, bookcases

Special Features: Coed, Z-rooms

James Hall

Profile: Low Rise, Phone, Cable TV, Ethernet, Several lounges, Kitchen with adjacent eating area, Laundry and vending machines

Typical Room Dimensions: 12' by 18' ft, single/bunkable or loftable beds, bookcases

Special Features: All-female, Z-rooms

Kennedy Hall

Profile: High Rise Tower, Phone, Cable TV, Ethernet, Study lounges on each floor, Kitchens on three floors, Classrooms, Club Kennedy (a student-run recreation floor with TV, Arcade and table games, and snack food, Laundry facilities on several floors, Vending machine on first floor

Typical Room Dimensions: 13' by 12.75 ft (corner rooms), single/bunkable beds, bookcases

Special Features: Coed, Single sex by floor, Z-rooms

Melville Hall

Profile: Low Rise, Phone, Cable TV, Ethernet, Kitchen with adjacent eating area, Lounges on every floor, Laundry and vending machines, Table games

Typical Room Dimension: 12' by 18' ft, single/bunkable or loftable beds, bookcases

Special Features: All-female residence, Z-rooms

Prince Hall

Profile: Low Rise, Phone, Cable TV, Ethernet, Lounges/study areas on several floors, some with TV's and one with a pool table, Large kitchen with cooking and dining facilities, Resident reading room, Laundry and vending machines

Typical Room Dimension: 12' by 18' ft, single/bunkable beds, bookcases

Special Features: Coed, Graduate student housing, 12-month housing option

Thoreau Hall

Profile: Low Rise, Phone, Cable TV, Ethernet, Kitchen, Several lounges, Laundry and vending machines

Typical Room Dimensions: Z-rooms, single/bunkable beds, bookcases

Special features: Coed

Cance Hall

Profile: Low Rise, Phone, Cable TV, Ethernet, Community lounges on each floor, Kitchen, First floor lounge with TV/pool table/foosball table, Laundry and vending machines

Typical Room Dimensions: 12' by 18' ft, single/bunkable or loftable beds, bookcases

Special Features: Coed, Talent Advancement Program for The Isenberg School of Management

John Adams Hall

Profile: High Rise Tower, Phone, Cable TV, Ethernet, Kitchens on three floors, Community lounge on each floor, Recreation room with TV, Classrooms, First floor lobby sitting area, Laundry and vending machines

Typical Room Dimensions: 13' by 12.75 ft (corner rooms), single/bunkable or loftable beds, bookcases

Special Features: Coed, Z-rooms, Talent Advancement Program for Communications, English, Psychology, Political Science

John Quincy Adams Hall

Profile: High Rise Tower, Phone, Cable TV, Ethernet, Community lounges on each floor, Kitchens on three floors, Club JQA (a student-run recreation floor with TV and table games), Laundry and vending machines

Typical Room Dimensions: 13' by 12.75 ft (corner rooms), single/bunkable beds, bookcases

Special Features: Coed, Wellness Center, 24-hour quiet floor

Mackimmie Hall

Profile: Low Rise, Phone, Cable TV, Ethernet, Community lounges on every floor, Kitchen with eating area, Recreation room with TV, Laundry and vending machines

Typical Room Dimensions: 12' by 18' ft, single/bunkable beds, bookcases

Special Features: Coed residence, some all-male floors, First year general education program

Moore Hall

Profile: Low Rise, Phone, Cable TV, Ethernet, Community lounges on every floor, Kitchen with eating area, Recreation room with TV, Classroom, Laundry and vending machines

Typical Room Dimensions: 12' by 18' ft, single/bunkable beds, bookcases

Special Features: Coed, Basement level all-male floor, First year general education program

Patterson Hall

Profile: Low Rise, Phone, Cable TV, Ethernet, Community lounges on every floor, Kitchen with eating area, Recreation room with TV, Laundry and vending machines

Typical Room Dimensions: 12' by 18' ft, single/bunkable beds, bookcases

Special Features: Coed, single sex by wing, First year general education program

Pierpont Hall

Profile: Low Rise, Phone, Cable TV, Ethernet, Community lounges one every floor, Kitchen with eating area, Recreation room with TV and pool table, Classroom, laundry and vending machines

Typical Room Dimensions: 12' by 18' ft, single/bunkable beds, bookcases

Special Features: Coed, one all-male floor, First year general education program

Washington Hall

Profile: High Rise Tower, Phone, Cable TV, Ethernet, Kitchens on three floors, Community lounges on every floor, Recreation room with TV and pool table, Classrooms, Laundry and vending machines

Typical Room Dimensions: 13' by 12.75 ft (corner rooms), single/bunkable beds, bookcases

(Washington Hall, continued)

Special Features: Coed, Wellness Center, Talent Advancement Program (Biology, Computer Science, Environmental Sciences, Mathematics, Nursing, Physical Sciences

Dormitory Cluster: Sylvan Overview:

"Sylvan Residence Area, the newest area just up the hill from Northeast, offers suite-style living in a shady wooded area. Each residence hall contains 64 suites and each suite is either all-male or all-female. Each suite is a mixture of double and single rooms, a common bathroom, and a common living room. Suites accommodate from six to eight residents."

The following 4 dorms are in Sylvan

Dorm

Phone, Cable TV, Ethernet, Main lounge with TV, Kitchen, Recreation room with pool table and other table games, Laundry and vending machines

Typical Room Dimensions: 14' by 10' ft, single/bunkable or loftable beds, bookcases

Special Features: Coed, single sex suites

Cashin Hall

Profile: Phone, Cable TV, Ethernet, Main lounge with TV, Kitchen, Recreation room with pool table, Laundry and vending machines

Typical Room Dimensions: 10' by 14' ft, single/bunkable or loftable beds, bookcases

Special Features: Coed, Single sex suites, Wellness Center, Sylvan Cultural Center, Area government office

MacNamara Hall

Profile: Phone, Cable TV, Ethernet, Kitchen, Recreation room with pool table, Main lounge with TV, Student-run snack bar with eating facilities, Laundry and vending machines

Typical Room Dimensions: 10' by 14' ft, single/bunkable or loftable beds, bookcases

Special Features: Coed, Single sex suites

Dormitory Cluster: Orchard Hill Overview:

"Overlooking campus, amid rolling hills and apple orchards, is the Orchard Hill Residential Area. The area consists of four residence halls surrounding a central grassy area known as 'The Bowl'. Each residence hall has seven floors with two corridors on each floor branching off from the lobby/elevator area in the center of the floor."

The following 4 dorms are in Orchard Hill:

Dickinson Hall

Profile: Phone, Cable TV, Ethernet, Study lounges on most floors, Kitchen on main level, Recreation room with pool table and color TV, Laundry and vending machines

Typical Room Dimensions: 12' by 16' ft, single/bunkable beds, bookcases

Special Features: Coed, Martin Luther King jr. Cultural Center, First-year engineering, Commonwealth College learning communities

Field Hall

Profile: Phone, Cable TV, Ethernet, Study lounges on most floors, Kitchens on three floors, Recreation room with pool table and TV, Field Snack Bar, Large community lounge on first floor, Laundry and vending machines

Typical Room Dimensions: 12' by 16' ft, single/bunkable beds, bookcases

Special Features: Coed, Orchard Hill are student government offices, Wellness floor, Commonwealth College learning communities, Faculty member in residence

Grayson Hall

Profile: Phone, Cable TV, Ethernet, Study lounges on most floors, Large main lounge, Kitchen, TV room, Laundry and vending machines

Typical Room Dimensions: 12' by 16' ft, single/bunkable or loftable beds, bookcases

Special Features: Coed, One all-female floor, Faculty member in residence, Commonwealth College learning communities

Webster Hall

Profile: Phone, Cable TV, Ethernet, Study lounges on most floors, Kitchens on three floors, Main lounge with piano, Recreation room with TV and pool table, Laundry and vending machines

Typical Room Dimensions: 12' by 16' ft, single/bunkable beds, bookcases

Special Features: Coed, Wellness Center, Faculty member in residence, Commonwealth College learning communities

Bed Type:

Twin extra long (39"x80")

some lofts

some bunk-beds

Available for Rent:

Mini fridge with microwave

Cleaning Service?

Bathrooms and hallways, almost every day

You Get:

Closet/wardrobe, bookcases, cesk, chair, Cable TV, Ethernet, local phone, dresser, window shade

Also Available:

Single sex, special interest options

Did You Know?

According to a survey taken; **"Students are so lazy that most pee in the shower,"** from Lazystudents. com, 75 percent of the 840 college students polled answered "yes" to an online question asking, "Do you pee in the shower?" In other words, bring flip-flops.

Students Speak Out On...
On-Campus Housing

"Orchard Hill is for a more studious crowd, Sylvan has a random mix of people, Northeast has a large Asian population with some hippies, and Central mostly appeals to earthy hippies. People were really cool in Southwest, where I lived. Lots of people from here join sororities, where they have good parties. There's a cute pond called Puffers that we all go to!"

Q "There are five areas on campus: Central, Southwest, Sylvan, Northeast and Orchard Hill. I have lived in Central for three years and think that **it is the nicest area** on campus. Northeast and Orchard Hill are also pretty nice. I'd avoid Sylvan because the rooms can get a little small, and Southwest because it's just a lot of concrete stairwells and such, which kind of creeps me out."

Q "The dorms are decent, but **stay away from Sylvan**. Southwest is my personal favorite, but only to visit. Sylvan is suite-style, so you're living with five or six other people. Southwest is a huge, concrete mess—the general rule of thumb is that you go to there to party, but not to live. I've lived in Central all three years and I loved it. It's located near just about everything, and the dorms are nice and made of brick."

Q "Northeast has the biggest and cleanest dorms, but **the social life really sucks**. It's far away from everything, so if you like a fun, social life and a clean dorm, or you want to be close to everything, live in Southwest in a low rise. Be sure you don't live in a tower, because they suck."

Q "Sylvan sucks, Northeast is quiet, and Orchard Hill is nice and quiet. **Central has a bit of a drug culture**, but they're very open minded and laid back. Southwest is big party area with tall towers, and the people there are pretty shallow. I lived in a low rise in Southwest for two years and I thought it was pretty fun. I will probably be an RA in Central in a year or so, because Central is pretty cool."

Q "The dorms aren't as bad as people make them out to be. **They are a little small**, but living there is a great way to meet people."

Q "**Some dorms are nice and some are not**. There are five areas, each with a distinct feel to them. Southwest is the urban center of campus. There are five high-rises going up twenty-two floors and eleven low-rises with four floors each. About a quarter of the students at UMass live there. I think it's supposed to be the most densely populated city block in the world, but it doesn't seem crowded. I live there, and it's a lot of fun. At least once during the year, there is a riot in Southwest—not even people breaking everything, but just celebrations when the Patriots or Red Sox win or when the Yankees lose. Everyone here hates the Yankees."

Q "Sylvan and Orchard Hill are for studying, so **live in Southwest or Central if you want to party**."

Q "Northeast and Central are the places to live because **the rooms are decent and not to far away from classes**. Aside from the distance, Orchard Hill is also a nice place to live. Don't live in Southwest because you might get stuck in a tower, and imagine trying to bring your computer up twenty-four floors. Almost every building has some sort of specialty like learning centers, classrooms, computer labs, or a snack bar, so figure out what you want."

The College Prowler Take On...
On-Campus Housing

UMass has five major clusters of dormitories. Each cluster has buildings that are worth avoiding either because the rooms are too small, or because you won't be able to get work done in your room. Overall, Central and Orchard Hill have the best dorms, although, Southwest has rooms called "Z rooms" that are worth checking out. Living in one of the Southwest towers can be a grueling experience, depending on what floor. One problem with living in either Sylvan or Orchard Hill is the long walk it takes to get to any classes. On the other hand, there are bus stops everywhere on campus, riding them is free and they come just about every five minutes. Northeast is nice because they have a sand volleyball court out in the quad, and once spring hits everyone goes outside to socialize.

UMass is good about placing students in the buildings that they requested. Unfortunately, because UMass enrolls more students than there is room for, freshmen will rarely, and only under special circumstances, get a single. Not to mention that when the dorm rooms run out, a handful of students have to stay in the Campus Center Hotel until a spot opens up. Most dorms have TV rooms and a pool table if you get bored or need a break from studying. Living on campus is a good way to make friends at a large school like UMass, you are sure to meet some interesting people. Because UMass is such a party school, the bathrooms on the weekends are absolutely disgusting. Everyone you talk to about college will tell you to bring flip-flops, and I would like to take this opportunity to reinforce that point. Much of how you perceive living on campus has to do with your roommate, so if you get stuck with someone whose behavior isn't congruent with your own, change rooms immediately and keep your fingers crossed.

B-

The College Prowler™ Grade on
Campus Housing: B-

A high Campus Housing grade indicates that dorms are clean, well-maintained, and spacious. Other determining factors include variety of dorms, proximity to classes, and social atmosphere.

Off-Campus Housing

The Lowdown On...
Off-Campus Housing

Undergrads in Off-Campus Housing:
41%

Average Rent for a 1BR Apartment:
$675-$800 per month

Average Rent for a 2BR Apartment:
$800-$1000 per month

For Assistance Contact:
Commuter Services and Housing Resource Center
Web: http://www-ims.oit.umass.edu/~cshrc/
Phone: (413) 545-0865
Fax: (413) 545-3633
E-mail: cshrc@stuaf.umass.edu

Amherst Apartment Complexes:

Alpine Commons
Telephone: (413) 256-0741
Distance to UMass: 2 miles
Studio: $575
1 Bedroom: N/A
2 Bedroom: $800
3 Bedroom: $1,355
4 Bedroom: $2,000
What's Included: Heat/HW/Elec

Aspen Chase
Telephone: (413) 256-0741
Distance to UMass: 1.5
Studio: N/A
1 Bedroom: $675-740
2 Bedroom: $860-945
3 Bedroom: $1,300
4 Bedroom: N/A
What's included? Heat/HW/Elec/Laundry

Brandywine
Telephone: (413) 549-0600
Distance to UMass: 1 mile
Studio: N/A
1 Bedroom: $755-785
2 Bedroom: $975-1,005
3 Bedroom: N/A
4 Bedroom: N/A
What's Included: Heat/HW

The Boulders
Telephone: (413) 256-8534
Distance to UMass: 2.5 miles
Studio: N/A

The Boulders, (continued...)
1 bedroom: N/A
2 Bedroom: $950
3 Bedroom: N/A
4 Bedroom: N/A
What's Included: Heat/HW/Laundry

Colonial Village
Telephone: (413) 253-2515
Distance to UMass: 2.5
Studio: N/A
1 Bedroom: $525-630
2 Bedroom: $655-760
3 Bedroom: N/A
4 Bedroom: N/A
What's Included: HW/Laundry

Puffton Village
Telephone: (413) 549-0145
Distance to UMass: 1 mile
Studio: N/A
1 Bedroom: $695-750
2 Bedroom: $900-995
3 Bedroom: $$1,150-1,275
4 Bedroom: N/A
What's Included: Heat/HW/Laundry

Village Park
Telephone: (413) 549-0099
Distance to UMass: 1 mile
Studio: N/A
1 Bedroom: $497
2 Bedroom: $623
3 Bedroom: $789
4 Bedroom: N/A
What's Included: Heat/HW/Laundry

Students Speak Out On...
Off-Campus Housing

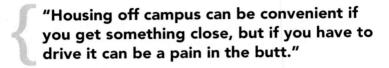

{ **"Housing off campus can be convenient if you get something close, but if you have to drive it can be a pain in the butt."**

Q "Housing off campus is pretty easy to find. There are lots of houses. **There are lots of off-campus options**, and some are even cheaper than living on campus. Most are right on the bus routes, making it easy to get to campus."

Q "Off-campus housing is pretty good. There are a lot of places to choose from, but **you have to really try hard** to get a place. They are affordable for the most part—if you are in a four-bedroom place with four people, it will probably run you about $350 - $400 a month."

Q "**Most junior and senior students live off campus**, where there are several apartment complexes. Most are less than a mile from campus and right on the bus route."

Q "Housing off campus is somewhat hard to find, but all of it is very close to campus. **If you don't have a car**, there are buses that will take you right to your living area, whether you live in North Amherst, South Amherst, Northampton, or Sunderland."

Q "There are many options for off-campus housing, but **you can't move off campus until junior year**. There are plenty of nice places to live at a very affordable price if you plan on doing it. There are plenty of parties out there, too."

Q "You're required to live on campus your first two years at UMass. After that, most people choose to move off campus. **There are tons of affordable apartment**s, houses, and condos either within walking distance of campus or on the bus route."

Q "We pay $1800 for an off-campus three-room apartment right in the center of town. **There are cheaper places**, if that seems too pricey."

Q "**If you are smart**, off-campus housing can be much cheaper than living in the dorms."

Q "Most of the places off campus are right on the bus route, so you never really need a car at UMass. The only thing you need to worry about is **getting roommates that are right for you**, and that doesn't necessarily mean your friends-believe me."

The College Prowler Take On...
Off-Campus Housing

Off-campus housing is very similar to living in the dorms except that you get a bathroom and kitchen that you share with three people as opposed to thirty. Actually, if you get off the meal plan and move off campus after your freshman and sophomore year, it can be much cheaper. On the down side, you have to worry about the hassle of getting to class, which basically leaves you with two options. You can either take the bus, which is relatively convenient, or drive your own car, which is relatively inconvenient. The parking lots are far from the classrooms and you have to purchase a parking permit. Brandywine is a nice off-campus place to live, but you can also find apartments that are both near UMass and on the bus route, a very convenient situation. Another option, that won't leave much in your bank account, is to get a house, an alternative that sometimes requires more than four roommates.

Some of the apartment complexes get just as crazy on the weekends as do the dorms, with the occasional "Yankees suck" riot. On the other hand, some of the housing complexes are quiet and occupied by more families than actual students. I was lucky enough to live in a beautiful and affordable apartment above a liquor store in Sunderland, so don't limit your search to places like Puffton, Brandywine, and The Boulders. The biggest issue with living off campus is transportation. If you have a car, and don't mind long walks, or if you live on the bus route, then you've got it made in the shade with pink lemonade.

The College Prowler™ Grade on

Off-Campus
Housing: C

A high grade in Off-Campus Housing indicates that apartments are of high quality, close to campus, affordable, and easy to secure.

Diversity

The Lowdown On...
Diversity

American Indian:
0.3%

Hispanic:
3.2%

Asian or Pacific Islander:
9.1%

White:
81.9%

African American:
4.8%

International:
1.1%

Political Activity

The town of Amherst, including the students from the University of Massachusetts, is a very politically active place. Most people here are of the liberal persuasion and will not hesitate to discuss or argue any important issue. Many political candidates campaign throughout the year at the various UMass auditoriums. The Student Government Association (SGA) has a very strong presence on campus and is known for effectively involving students.

Gay Tolerance

The homosexual community at UMass is quite prevalent. Once a year a rally is held at the Student Union to discuss issues pertaining to their lifestyle. In fact, Mary Lyon Hall in The Northeast residential area has a 2-20 floor where gay, lesbian, bisexual, and transgender students can choose to live. Also, The Stonewall Center (413-545-4824), a gay, lesbian, bisexual, and transgender educational resource center, offers various information that caters to the homosexual community.

Economic Status

Just about every economic class is represented at UMass. At any given moment you could see an El Camino and a Lincoln Navigator stopped at the same red light. The students at nearby Amherst College are very affluent, while UMass students, on average, illustrate a more accurate depiction of middle-class America.

Minority Clubs

The office of A.L.A.N.A. Affairs (African, Latino/a, Asian/ Pacific Islander, and Native American) is a multicultural and educational support agency that exists to serve the needs of UMass's minority population. Universal access to education is a strong theme at UMass, and groups such as A.L.A.N.A. work towards reaching that goal. A.L.A.N.A. is a conglomeration of over twenty minority clubs that remain very active on campus by holding rallies, speeches, and other events to address and solve any problems facing students of an ethnic minority. A.L.A.N.A. can be reached online at http://www.umass.edu/ alana/.

Most Popular Religions:

If there is a "popular" religion on campus it is probably Christianity, however, there are many registered student organizations on campus that reflect a few of the other religions. These groups can be found on the UMass website at http://www.umass.edu/religious_affairs, and include:

- Alliance Christian Fellowship
- Athletes in Action
- Campus Crusade for Christ
- Chabad House
- Christian Faculty Ministry
- Episcopal Chaplaincy
- First Baptist Church
- Hillel House
- Intervarsity Christian fellowship
- Jewish Affairs
- Mercy House
- Muslim Students Association
- Navigators Christian Ministry
- United Christian foundation
- Upside down/ International Church of Christ.

Despite the number of religious groups religion plays a minor role at UMass and is not exceptionally visible on campus.

Students Speak Out On...
Diversity

> "The campus is really diverse. You can learn a lot from other people, racially and culturally, if you make an effort to do so."

Q "**Groups tend to form around people** from the same ethnic groups. It's understandable, but with more diversity, there would be more unity."

Q "You are almost guaranteed to meet someone from every race at UMass. **You'll meet many people** from different cultures—it's great. There are several groups for different cultural backgrounds and sexual orientations, and any type of discrimination is totally unacceptable! Be prepared to come to UMass with an open mind."

Q "**Black, white, gay, straight, or whatever**—there is something for everyone here."

Q "I come from a white suburban town, and **UMass definitely opened up my eyes** to all kinds of different races and ethnicities—it's awesome!"

Q "Diversity was somewhat of an issue before the budget cuts came along. **The minorities on campus had rallies** last year, saying not enough minorities were accepted into UMass. It seems to me like there is plenty of diversity, though."

Q "The diversity on this campus is a point of pride. There are all kinds of people and **very little blatant racism**. People are cool with most crowds out here."

Q "I have met **many people from different countries** that go to UMass, and have made a lot of friends as a result. UMass is a predominantly white community, but you really don't have to go far to experience diversity."

Q "At a big school like this you are bound to have classmates and teachers that are from another country. **Most people here are very accepting** of foreigners, but some people have a very narrow view of the world. I'm sure that those people can be found in any country though."

Q "UMass really **forced me to see the world**."

The College Prowler Take On...
Diversity

UMass is fairly diverse, and there are many cultural groups to get involved with on campus. I have met and become friends with many people from different countries at UMass, and I have yet to observe or experience any type of racism. The quality of education at any school increases with the level of diversity, and UMass definitely benefits from this reality. Professors here frequently take advantage of this situation to explore the relevancy of others cultures on our own lives. I believe September 11th really served as a catalyst in this respect. Although predominantly a white population, twenty-eighth different countries were represented by the students at my graduation.

Women slightly outnumber men at UMass, so no one should have an excuse. One ethnically exclusive group on campus, whether deliberate or not, is the Honor's Commonwealth College. This group has been deemed "elitist" by many a Daily Collegian article and is comprised mainly of Caucasian students. I myself was a member during my sophomore year and saw little benefit, educational or otherwise, aside from being given a yellow rope to wear when you graduate. The exposure you obtain to different ways of life at UMass often catches new students by surprise. The diversity this campus offers in the middle of such a non-diverse region is an important theme here at UMass.

The College Prowler™ Grade on
Diversity: C-

A high grade in Diversity indicates that ethnic minorities and international students have a notable presence on campus and that students of different economic backgrounds, religious beliefs, and sexual preferences are well-represented.

Guys & Girls

The Lowdown On...
Guys & Girls

Men Undergrads:	Women Undergrads:
49%	51%

Birth Control Available?
Yes. University Health Services, Resident Assistants

Hookups or Relationships?
The wide array of personalities at any school really makes this topic subjective. If you are looking for your future husband/wife at a frat party, I wish you all the luck in the world. Then again, if you are looking for just one night of company, you probably won't find him/her in the library. As an estimated guess, I would say that roughly seventy-five percent of the relationships that begin at UMass are not altogether serious, and therefore end at UMass.

Best Place to Meet Guys/Girls:

The best place to meet guys and girls is in the dorms where you live, and usually on the same floor. The number of relationships that have resulted from this scenario far exceeds any other. Another good place to meet guys and girls is in class, but at least pretend that you went there to take notes. Parties, because they are usually huge, are host to more single people than you can shake a stick at. UMass is crammed with attractive people which you could look at as a good thing because of all the variety, or a bad thing because of all the competition.

Social Scene:

Contrary to what you might expect from a big school, students at UMass can easily form groups of close friends and network to all areas of campus. Because of a common living situation or class schedule students often find themselves interacting with the same people on a daily basis. In general, the people enrolled at UMass are very friendly, and as freshmen are probably just as eager to make new friends as you are.

Dress Code

All shapes and sizes. Although, I think the frat guys have a mandatory Abercrombie and Fitch dress code.

Did You Know?

Top Places to Find Hotties:
- Classes
- Parties
- Athletic Events

Top Places to Hookup:
- In your dreams
- Your roommate's bed
- Their roommate's bed

Students Speak Out On...
Guys & Girls

"People at UMass range from hippies to frat guys to jocks to nerds—anything you can think of. There are a lot of attractive people here, and I'm sure you could find someone that suits your taste."

Q "It's your general college campus, with **a wide variety of people** around."

Q "**We're a pretty good-looking campus**, but beauty is only skin deep. There are lots of ditzy girls and jock boys who completely fill the stereotypes, but there are also plenty of good-looking, nice people, too."

Q "There are so many guys that it's always easy to find one you like. In my case, I see a new hot guy every day! **It's always nice to look**. I have mixed feelings about the girls here—some are cool, but some are snotty."

Q "For the most part, everyone I've met at UMass is great. You meet so many different people, and **everyone has their own lifestyle**. It's amazing. There's a huge amount of attractive people everywhere."

Q "There are people from all walks of life and with many different personalities on campus. I'm sure you won't have any trouble making friends. There are a lot of good-looking people here, but of course there are some ugly ones, too. **Everyone is very accepting, though**."

Q "Personally, **I never had any trouble finding attractive guys** on campus. There are jocks, hippies, and gangster types. Depending on what area of campus you live in, you'll probably be exposed to different types of people. In general, UMass has a pretty attractive population."

Q "**You'll find your ghetto folk**, your rich brats, your hippies, and your nerds. The diversity on this campus is one of its high points. Any kind of person could come here and find a group of people to fit in with."

Q "UMass women are very easy on the eyes, and **they are a dime a dozen**. Most of them have their heads on straight, but some you'd swear do not belong in college."

Q "I think because this school is so big a lot of people try especially hard to stick out by wearing ridiculous clothes or hardly any at all. **This place is crawling with attractive people**, what am I doing inside?"

The College Prowler Take On...
Guys & Girls

Without a doubt, UMass has some remarkable student bodies with more than its share of attractive people. More women than men enroll at UMass every year, so for guys the odds are looking pretty good. If, however, you want to see a lot of people who all dress, talk, and behave the same way, I suggest any frat or sorority. By simply walking around campus, one can observe some beautiful scenery. Dozens of possibilities exist for meeting people, and maybe it's just me, but, doesn't it always seem to happen when you least expect it?

On a scale from one to ten of sexual promiscuity, one being a convent and ten being a brothel, I'd say UMass ranks about a seven or eight. Random hookups happen here all the time, and judging from personal experience, they happen to people who forgot to register for "closing window shades 101", a valuable course. On the whole, everywhere you go people are generally the same with a few exceptions, every stereotypical guy and girl can be found here in great numbers. A valid concern your parents may have about sending their child to UMass is that you are going to focus more on getting phone numbers than good grades, welcome to college.

The College Prowler™ Grade on Guys: A-

A high grade for Guys indicates that the male population on campus is attractive, smart, friendly, and engaging, and that the school has a decent ratio of guys to girls.

The College Prowler™ Grade on Girls: A-

A high grade for Girls not only implies that the women on campus are attractive, smart, friendly, and engaging, but also that there is a fair ratio of girls to guys.

Athletics

The Lowdown On...
Athletics

Athletic Division:
NCAA Division 1

Conference:
Atlantic 10
Hockey East

Males Playing Varsity Sports:
316 (3%)

Females Playing Varsity Sports:
292 (2%)

Men's Varsity Sports
Alpine Skiing
Baseball
Basketball
Cross Country
Diving
Football
Ice Hockey
Lacrosse
Soccer
Swimming
Tennis
Track and Field

➜

Women's Varsity Sports:

Alpine Skiing
Basketball
Crew
Cross Country
Diving
Field Hockey
Lacrosse
Soccer
Softball
Swimming
Tennis
Track and Field(Indoor)
Track and Field(Outdoor)

Club Sports:

Bicycle racing
Fencing
Lacrosse
Rowing
Rugby
Volleyball

Women's Club Sports:

Bicycle racing
Fencing
Ice hockey
Rugby

Intramurals:

Basketball
Field hockey
Flag football
Ice hockey
Soccer
Softball
Swimming
Tennis
Track and field
Ultimate frisbee
Volleyball
Walleyball
Wrestling

School Mascot

Minuteman

Most Popular Sports

Basketball and football

Getting Tickets

Free for students, as long as you show up with your
student ID.

Best Place to Take a Walk

There is a bike path that starts at Southwest and goes all over Amherst, Campus pond, center of town

Athletic Fields

Intramural Soccer/softball/football/field hockey fields, Baseball field, Tennis courts, Football practice field, Curry Hicks Field, Warren P. McGuirk Alumni Stadium, Soccer field

Gyms/Facilities

Boyden Gym

Boyden Gymnasium has two weight rooms, fitness center, Olympic-sized swimming pool, 3 handball courts, 2 walleyball courts, 6 basketball courts, 4 badminton courts, 4 volleyball courts, gymnastics center, and squash/paddleball courts. This gym is in fair condition and is closest to the Southwest Residential living area. The weight rooms have very limited hours of operation and are therefore perpetually crowded.

Curry Hicks

The Curry Hicks building has a good pool, and is located close to Boyden Gym. This facility is not to be confused with Curry Hicks Field that has artificial turf and is used by the lacrosse and softball team among others.

Totman Gym

Totman Gym is close to Northeast and Sylvan Residential living areas. They also have a pool, 2 basketball courts, badminton courts, volleyball courts, and a very dilapidated fitness center. Although large, this facility probably has the most inadequate equipment of any on campus.

Students Speak Out On...
Athletics

> "Football and basketball are the biggest varsity sports on campus. Intramural (IM) sports are very popular, too. They are a great way to make friends, and have some fun."

Q "**Basketball is huge**. Other sports like lacrosse, soccer, softball, and baseball are very competitive but don't get too much attention. Hockey is okay. As far as intramural sports go, they are huge! There are tons of different sports to play for both semesters."

Q "Varsity sports are fairly big on-campus, but **not as big as they used to be**. UMass basketball was once quite the event, but they have definitely tailed off in recent years."

Q "The football team sucks, and **not many people go to see the games**. If they do, it's to see the marching band—no joke. The marching band is incredible! I'm not too sure about intramural sports, because a lot of them were recently eliminated because of the budget cuts."

Q "Sports are very big on campus, but **they have come under the knife with the budget cuts**. Everyone loves football, and Midnight Madness, the first night the basketball team starts practice for the season, is a big deal. Our teams really aren't that good, even with our enthusiasm."

Q "**Sports are doing the best** with all the budget cuts happening here, better than the academics anyway."

Q "Five or so years ago the basketball team made it to the NCAA Final Four and lost to Kentucky. They're not as good right now, but **the program has hardly shrunk**. The football team was Division II National Champs a few years back and continues to do well. Girl's softball is dominating and actually set an NCAA record this past year with about thirty wins in a row. Baseball and soccer do okay, too."

Q "I play two intramural sports every semester and love it. This year we won the softball tournament which had like sixty-four teams! **Varsity sports aren't as big** as they once were, which means that you can get awesome seats to just about any game. I think Doctor-J went to school here."

Q "**UMass has a lot of nationally competitive varsity teams** that practically no one knows about. People only care about the men's basketball and football teams. The Red Sox are more popular here than the Minutemen."

The College Prowler Take On...
Athletics

Surprisingly, varsity sports on campus are not very big, especially when compared to Universities of similar size like UConn or some Boston schools. A lot of the less popular sports are now done away with, and you'll never have a problem finding a seat at a football or basketball game. On the plus side, all tickets for sporting events are free for students. Conversely, Intramural sports are big, and a great distraction from homework. I played both Intramural soccer and softball and had a great time.

The athletic facilities on campus are decent, but nothing to write home about. If you play a varsity sport then you'll have access to very nice gyms with much newer equipment. The Mullins Center is a beautiful arena, and the surrounding athletic fields, which include all of the intramural fields, are also in good shape. The person who spoke in the last quote accurately stated that the Red Sox are more popular here than the Minutemen. UMass has a large Boston influence, and most of the enthusiasm displayed by students gets directed towards Boston teams. Until the situation with the budget cuts improves, I only predict a further decline of quality at UMass in terms of athletics.

B

The College Prowler™ Grade on
Athletics: B

A high grade in Athletics indicates that students have school spirit, that sports programs are respected, that games are well-attended, and that intramurals are a prominent part of student life.

Nightlife

The Lowdown On...
Nightlife

Club and Bar Prowler:
Popular Nightlife Spots!

The clubs in Amherst are awful, they are tiny and don't offer much in the way of music. If you have your heart set on a club, I recommend you go to Holyoke, Northampton, or Springfield. Springfield has a great club called the Hippodrome that a lot of UMass students go to.

Atlantis
41 Boltwood Walk
Amherst Center
(413) 253-0025
Atlantis is one of only two clubs in Amherst, the other being The Pub. Atlantis operates as a restaurant during the day and a club at night on the weekends. The food there is good and I think the interior decorator may have a drug problem.

➡

The Pub
15 East Pleasant St.
Amherst Center
(413) 549-1200

The Pub is the other club in Amherst that is also a restaurant by day. This place gets pretty packed on the weekends, and you don't have to be twenty-one to get in. You also should dress accordingly when going to The Pub, so leave your overalls at home.

Amherst has a lot of bars, most of which are good. The Bluewall is the only bar on campus, a good place to go if you don't want to risk driving home. The center of Amherst is always lively on the weekends and worth checking out because of all the bars, which also makes it a great place to go bar hopping.

Amherst Brewing Company
24 North Pleasant St
Amherst, Ma
(413) 253-4400

Barsie's
43 North Pleasant St.
Amherst, Ma
(413) 256-1404

Charlie's
1 Pray St.
Amherst, Ma
(413) 549-5403

China Dynasty
351 Northampton Rd.
Amherst, Ma
(413) 256-8800

Delano's
57 North Pleasant St.
Amherst, Ma
(413) 253-5141

Elijah Boltwood's Tavern
30 Boltwood Ave
Amherst, Ma
(413) 253-2576

Monkey Bar & Grill
63 North Pleasant St.
Amherst, Ma
(413) 259-1600

Old Amherst Ale House
460 West St.
Amherst, Ma
(413) 256-1710

Peking Garden
48 Russell St
Hadley, Ma
(413) 586-1202

Pruddy's Tropical Bar & Grill
30 Boltwood Walk
Amherst, Ma
(413) 253-3345

Rafter's
422 Amity St.
Amherst, Ma
(413) 549-4040

Chili's Bar & Grill
426 Russell St.
Hadley, Ma
(413) 253-4008

**Applebee's Neighborhood
Bar & Grill**
100 Westgate Center Dr.
Hadley, Ma
(413) 253-5799

Primary Areas with Nightlife:
Amherst Center
Frat Row
Dormitories
Apartment complexes

Cheapest Place to Get a Drink:
Frat Party ($5.00 all you can drink)

Favorite Drinking Games:
Beer Pong
Card Games (A$$hole)
Century Club
Quarters
Power Hour
Up river-Down river
Bull Sh*t

What to Do if You're Not 21:

I'd say get a fake ID but they don't work around here. All of the alcohol-serving businesses are well aware of the fact that most college students are under the age of twenty-one. The frats, if you really want to, let underage people in all the time. Also, you can get away with drinking in your dorm or at an apartment if you're under 21. But of course, since all of these things are illegal, I do not recommend them. Your best bet is to head to Northampton and catch a live show, or any one of a million things that don't involve booze.

Organization Parties:

All of the athletic teams on campus, varsity and intramural, throw parties regularly. Many of them are located at houses where members of the team live, or at local bars and restaurants. Most every registered student organization throws a party at least once a year. Most of the parties thrown by UMass clubs are open to everyone, although some require membership of some form.

Frats:

See the Greek Section!

Students Speak Out On...
Nightlife

"All of the bars all have different styles. Once the bars let out, a wicked lot of people go to Antonio's and get food or chill on the sidewalk. It's always a good time. There are clubs in Northampton and in Springfield that I have heard are pretty decent."

"**We have a great strip for bars**, with Barsie's, Monkey Bar, and Delano's right in a row. They are all great places. You can also go to China Dynasty or Peking Garden if you're willing to try to get away with a really bad fake."

"Uptown is very popular for the over-twenty-one crowd. Amherst has several bars like Monkey Bar, Charlie's, The Pub, and Delano's. The Pub is a dance place, **often open for everyone 18-and-older**. We also have Klub Kai and Pearl Street--two clubs that have become less popular in the past year but are still favorites. Springfield, about forty-five minutes away, has a popular dance place called the Hippodrome."

"Downtown Amherst has a huge bar scene. **You can hit 'club sidewalk'** after all the bars get out everyone hangs out on the sidewalk and chills."

"Going to bars in Amherst is pretty tough if you're underage, **unless you have an awesome fake ID**. In the two years I was at UMASS, I only got into a bar once with a fake, and I ended up getting busted anyway. If you're lucky enough to meet security people, there are definitely ways to get in."

Q "There's a kind of sketchy converted Chinese food place called Klub Kai, but **it can be really ghetto at times**. The football team hosts parties there a lot."

Q "The Monkey Bar gets a lot of people on Thursday and Friday nights, but **the hot spot seems to be Atlantis**. By day it's a restaurant and lounge, and by night it's the most hopping club outside of Northampton. In Northampton, there's the Pearl Street Night Club, the Calvin Theater, the Iron Horse Music Hall, and a few other bars with live entertainment or DJs."

Q "The Pub is a place in Amherst that is a restaurant by day and a club by night. The best part is that **you can go there even if you aren't twenty-one**."

Q "**The bars in Amherst are just expensive frat parties**, but sometimes that is better than nothing. UMass is great because you can just walk around and find a party any night of the week. Just remember to bring $5.00 because that is how much a cup usually costs."

Q "Everyone knows that **UMass parties are out of control**."

The College Prowler Take On...
Nightlife

Not only is the nightlife at UMass unlike anywhere else, but you can find a party just about any night of the week. Commonly used terms such as malted Mondays, toasted Tuesdays, wet Wednesdays, and thirsty Thursdays attest to the fact that UMass is a party school through and through. The bigger parties usually occur at the frat houses, off- campus apartments, and downtown Amherst, whereas the smaller parties (if you can call them that) generally happen in the dorms. There are many annual parties on and off campus like the Hobart Ho-down, many of which inevitably escalate into riots that you could set your watch to. The bars in Amherst are good, while the clubs are few and far between.

As made apparent from the quotes above, certain places are known for having the best parties, okay parties, or no parties at all. Southwest and central have very spirited parties on a rather frequent basis, while Orchard Hill and Sylvan aren't quite as fervent. The same holds true for the larger apartment complexes like Puffton, Brandywine, and The Boulders as compared to the smaller Colonial Village and Alpine Commons. The amount of alcohol that gets consumed at some of these parties is staggering. So if you do choose UMass, be prepared to change your entire sleeping schedule because you have never seen anything like this.

B

The College Prowler™ Grade on

Nightlife: B

A high grade in Nightlife indicates that there are many bars and clubs in the area that are easily accessible and affordable. Other determining factors include the number of options for the under-21 crowd and the prevalence of house parties.

Greek Life

The Lowdown On...
Greek Life

Number of Fraternities:
21 (11 houses)

Number of Sororities:
12 (7 houses)

Fraternities and Sororities on Campus:
Alpha Chi Omega
Alpha Delta Phi
Alpha Epsilon Phi
Alpha Epsilon Pi

Alpha Kappa Alpha
Alpha Phi Alpha
Alpha Tau Gamma
Chi Omega
Delta Sigma Theta
Delta Upsilon
Delta Xi Phi
Delta Zeta
Gamma Phi Sigma
Groove Phi Groove
Iota Gamma Upsilon
Iota Phi Theta
Kappa Alpha Psi

➜

Fraternities & Sororities
(continued ...)

Kappa Kappa Gamma
Kappa Phi Lambda
Lambda Phi Epsilon
Lambda Pi Chi
Lambda Upsilon Lambda
Omega Delta
Phi Beta Sigma
Phi Sigma Kappa
Pi Delta Psi
Pi Lambda Phi
Sigma Alpha Mu
Sigma Delta Tau
Sigma Gamma Rho
Sigma Phi Epsilon
Sigma Kappa
Sigma Lambda Upsilon
Sigma Psi Zeta
Sigma Tau Gamma
Theta Chi
Zeta Beta Tau

Other Greek Organizations

Greek Council
Greek Peer Advisors
Interfraternity Council
Order of Omega
Panhellenic Council

Multi-cultural colonies:

Multicultural Greek Council (comprised of: Gamma Phi Sigma, Pi Delta Psi, Lambda Pi Chi, Sigma Lambda Upsilon, Lambda Upsilon Lambda, Sigma Psi Zeta)

African Student Association
Afrik-Am
Ahora
Arab Students Association
Asian American Student Association
Black Student Union
Boricuas Unidos
Cambodian Student Association
Cape Verdean Student Alliance
Casa Dominicana
English Speaking Caribbean Association
Haitian American Students Association
Japan America Club
Jewish Student Union
Korean Student Association
Native America Students Association
Persian Student Organization
Pride Alliance
Russian Student Organization
Student Association for the Multicultural Brazilian Alliance
South Asian Students Association
Taiwanese Student Association
Vietnamese Student Association
Wazobia Group

Students Speak Out On...
Greek Life

"It's terrible to say, but it's the 'freshman thing' to do. The frat houses are a place for underage people to party and drink. Sororities are viewed as snobby, but I know plenty of girls in them who are sweethearts. Fraternities and sororities at UMass are definitely looked down upon, but the people who are in them love being Greek."

Q "Greek life is alright, but it's **mostly washed-up jocks and sluts**. Freshmen love it, but after your first year you kind of get sick of it. There are tons of parties at people's off-campus apartments, so once the fraternities lose their value, there are still parties to go to."

Q "The social scene at UMass is **dominated primarily by off-campus parties**. They aren't far—when they say 'off campus,' it usually means about two miles."

Q "Even though I am not in a fraternity, I'd say **Greek life plays a big role** in the campus community. Some of the brothers are always doing community service and are active in student government, but others are just there to drink their college lives away. If you intend to join a fraternity or sorority, you could probably find one that fits your lifestyle."

Q "I am in a sorority, and I'm so glad I joined. We have a wonderful house and a lot of great girls. **There are always a lot of activities going on**, plus lots of parties."

Q "There are **rumors about the Greek system** being eliminated within the next couple of years, so if you're really interested in joining a frat, you may want to research that before you decide to come to UMass. If you're not interested in going Greek, there's definitely not any pressure to do so."

Q "Fraternities and sororities are pretty good at making their presence known on campus because of all the community work they do. I almost joined a frat when I was a freshman, but **then I saw the frat houses** - complete dumps."

Q "There are plenty of other ways you can meet people and make friends at UMass other than being involved in Greek life. Each frat has a somewhat of a different theme, so **it really depends on what you are looking for.**"

The College Prowler Take On...
Greek Life

I wouldn't say that Greek life dominates the social scene, but it is a large part of it. Some of the frats and sororities are very involved with the local community and with school projects, and some are not. I remember going to the frats as a freshman during my very first weekend at UMass, and that was enough for me. For the amount of Greek organizations on campus you'd think they would be more visible, although, from time to time they will host an event and make their presence known.

I remember watching some frat brothers ride their bicycles off of a ramp into the Campus Pond one year—that was hilarious. The Pond is only about three feet deep in the middle, so they would all come out of the water with a serious limp. The frats have a long tradition at UMass, and joining one is a big commitment. Most likely, because there are so many, the frats at UMass play a larger role in campus life than most other Universities.

B+

The College Prowler™ Grade on
Greek Life: B+

A high grade in Greek Life indicates that sororities and fraternities are not only present, but also active on campus. Other determining factors include the variety of houses available and the respect the Greek community receives from the rest of the campus.

Drug Scene

The Lowdown On...
Drug Scene

Most Prevalent Drugs on Campus:
Marijuana
Alcohol

Drug Couanseling Programs

The Drug and Alcohol Education program offers general information, referrals, training and peer workshops and is located on campus through University Health Services. They can be reached at (413) 577-5181.

The Residential Education Alcohol program provides general information, referral, and multi-session alcohol education programs for UMass students. This program is located in the Moore lobby, for more information call (413) 545-0137.

Other drug and alcohol programs that occur on campus include; Alcoholics Anonymous (413-532-2111), Alanon (413-253-5261), Adult Children of Alcoholics/ Dysfunctional Families (413-545-2337), Narcotics Anonymous (413-538-7479).

Students Speak Out On...
Drug Scene

{ **"Drugs are decreasing in popularity on campus, but they'll probably always be present. The drug of choice is marijuana, but you will sometimes find acid, ecstasy, and amphetamines being used."**

Q "If you want something you can easily get it, but **there's no pressure to do drugs** or anything."

Q **"There are not too many drugs around**. The dorm area Central is the biggest area for the drug crowd, though it's also one of the nicest dorms. There's weed, shrooms, and acid—stuff like that, but it's mostly drinking."

Q "There's no peer pressure, and drugs are pretty private. If you do it, **everyone's fine with it**, but if you don't, you're fine, too. It's no big deal—there's no epidemic and there definitely isn't a drug problem."

Q "There's lots of pot but that's about it. **You'll run into Ecstasy here and there**, but it's not like we have coke heads or heroine addicts running around."

Q **"There's a big drug scene,** but it's easily avoidable."

Q "The drug scene on-campus is what you make it out to be. **It's definitely easy to get pot**, like at any college, but it's not overwhelming if you're not interested. Some parts of campus are known more for drug use than others."

Q "You can get **whatever you want.**"

Q "People love their herb out here—marijuana, if you're not down with the lingo. **I haven't seen too many hard drugs**, but they are there if you really want them."

Q "You can always find people who do what you're into. Just stay away from the people you need to. It's a huge place, so **it won't be hard to avoid things** you don't like. I haven't met too many people who have real problems with anything."

Q "If you are not involved in drugs you won't really see them, but **you will smell a lot of weed**."

Q "The drug scene here is very noticeable, especially the use of weed. A lot of people here smoke weed and it isn't hard to get. Once in a while you will see people doing coke or pills like oxycotton and vicadin at a party, but **it is all very avoidable**. Although, if you don't want to be around drugs I suggest not living in Southwest or Central."

The College Prowler Take On...
Drug Scene

To my knowledge, excessive drug use on campus has not recently been a concern. The UMass newspaper (The Daily Collegian) prints arrests that were made the day before, and the number one cause of arrests on campus is drugs (specifically, weed), whether student or non-student. Even so, the number of drug-related arrests on campus given the number of students is unexpectedly low. Drugs can be found at UMass, but in no way are they unavoidable. Once in a great while you may smell the odor of marijuana in a dormitory hallway, but almost never will you come across someone doing a harder drug. I don't know if this is because drug users at UMass are few, or because they are very clandestine about their behavior.

The Central Residence area has the most noticeable drug culture on campus, but Southwest is not far behind. The UMPD and Amherst Police department do their jobs well and consequently deter a lot of people from doing drugs. For instance, last semester a large drug bust was made in Southwest where police confiscated large quantities of drugs and money, and sure enough, the front page of the next day's Daily Collegian was completely devoted to covering this story. Tactics like that are just one of the ways police remind students that narcotics and weapons will not be tolerated on campus.

The College Prowler™ Grade on
Drug Scene: B-

A high grade in the Drug Scene indicates that drugs are not a noticeable part of campus life; drug use is not visible, and no pressure to use them seems to exist.

Campus Strictness

The Lowdown On...
Campus Strictness

What Are You Most Likely to Get Caught Doing on Campus? (According to the UMPD)

- Using a fake ID
- Possession of an open container of alcohol
- Driving with alcohol in your car when you are under 21
- Driving under the influence of drugs and/or alcohol
- Making a lot of noise in your apartment or dorm room
- Parking illegally

Students Speak Out On...
Campus Strictness

"You can drink and smoke all you like in your dorm, as long as you're not an idiot about it. Just towel your door, keep alcohol covered, and don't flaunt anything. The resident assistants know that most kids do illegal things, but as long as you don't make it obvious to them and keep relatively quiet, you can do whatever you want."

Q "Campus police are pretty understanding, but **the town police in Amherst are jerks**."

Q **"Police aren't too tolerant about drugs**, but they know we're all college students and are pretty laid-back about drinking. The dorms have policies prohibiting underage drinking in residential areas, but the policies are seldom enforced."

Q "You can get away with a lot. I've had several incidents on campus where I've been drinking and never got caught. If you do get caught, though, **the penalties are pretty severe**."

Q "The police say they're strict, but a lot of stuff goes on that they don't know about. **We're not a dry campus**, so if you're twenty-one you can bring a certain amount of alcohol into the dorms."

Q "Underage drinking on campus is kind of like drinking at your parent's house while they are away. **If they find out you're screwed**, but if not, it will be an awesome time."

Q "I've never known anyone to really get in trouble. If you do something blatantly illegal, like walk down frat row carrying liquor or try to sell drugs in the lobby of a dorm, you'll get arrested. **It's really easy not to get in trouble**, though."

Q "The police just want to make sure that **everyone is being safe** and will hopefully wake up the next day."

Q "You really have to try to get in trouble here. If you are doing something illegal, **there are many ways to avoid detection**. The RAs are relatively understanding, they are students too and don't want to be held responsible for someone hurting themselves or others on their floor. If you are lucky your room won't be right next to one."

Q "The people who are constantly causing problems are the ones who never get caught. **There is tons of drinking here**, and all the good stuff that goes along with it."

The College Prowler Take On...
Campus Strictness

UMass is not strict by any means. Certain behavior will get you in trouble if you get caught, and certain behavior may or may not get you in trouble if you get caught. The penalties for doing something serious like selling drugs are severe, but if you get caught with a beer in your room you might have to go to an alcohol education class. If you get caught again the punishment stiffens, and so on. But really, UMass authorities, including the RAs, keeping in mind they are also students, are good about focusing on what's important—safety. One thing RAs crack the whip about is playing with fire extinguishers that are located on each floor, so don't do that.

However, do not assume that behavior you can get away with on campus is behavior you can get away with at the frats, apartments, or anywhere else off campus. Amherst Police don't tolerate college students as much as UMass Police. Getting in deep trouble at UMass is like getting bad grades in really easy classes, you have to try. Another thing that is taken seriously on campus is stopping your car for pedestrians, a law that doesn't necessarily apply to people driving around off campus in Amherst. Every year I recall at least one person getting fatally hit by a car on campus. The fines are steep for neglecting this law, and it is not taken lightly. Unfortunately, during specific times of the day when classes are getting out, this means that you may have to sit at a crosswalk for a long time. In conclusion, campus strictness is not overwhelming at UMass by any means; the main concern is that students remain safe.

A-

The College Prowler™ Grade on
Campus Strictness: A-

A high Campus Strictness grade implies an overall lenient atmosphere; police and RAs are fairly tolerant, and the administration's rules are flexible.

Parking

The Lowdown On...
Parking

Approximate Parking Permit Cost
$145-225 for freshmen and sophomores

UMass Parking Services
Phone: (413) 545-0065
Fax: (413) 545-4440
Lot 25 Trailer Complex
51 Forestry Way
Amherst, Ma 01003
http://www-parking.admin.
umass.edu

Common Parking Tickets:
Expired Meter: $20
No Parking Zone: $40
Handicapped Zone: $100
Fire Lane: $40

Student Parking Lot?
Yes

Freshman Allowed to Park?
Yes

Parking Permits

Applying for a parking permit at UMass is relatively simple, you could go to their offices, call by phone, or visit their website. Their regular office hours are Mon-Fri 7:45am-4:30 p.m., and Mon-Fri 8:00 a.m.-3:45 p.m. during the off-session periods. The parking lots are designated by color, the yellow lots being the most undesirable because they are unpaved, crime ridden, and far away from everything. Freshmen and sophomores are restricted to the yellow, purple, and green lots which cost $145, $185, and $225, respectively. Another option is the campus garage; conveniently located at the center of campus, this option is probably the most expensive.

Did You Know?

Best Places to Find a Parking Spot

Depends on where you are going, they all have their drawbacks. If you live in the dorms then the best place to park is near your building, if possible.

Good Luck Getting a Parking Spot Here!

Fine Arts Center

It's easy to appeal a ticket at UMass, and your chances of being successful are actually pretty good. You can do so online at http://www-parking.admin.umass.edu/Appeals.

Students Speak Out On...
Parking

"The parking system sucks, especially for freshmen. The parking lots are far away, but you really won't use a car when you're on campus anyways. It's much easier to use the buses, which run about every ten minutes."

Q "My roommate and I have very few problems parking, but **it depends on how crowded it is** where you live and what year you are."

Q "As a freshman **you'll only be able to get a yellow lot sticker**, which means you'll have to park in the lots farthest from campus. It's a pain, and the lots aren't paved. The police also tend to tow people from there frequently."

Q "If you can avoid having a car the first year, I'd recommend it. **There's a free bus system** that goes to a lot of places, so it isn't necessary to have a car."

Q "Freshmen have to get Yellow Lot stickers, and although there is one really good lot, the other two are terrible. The **parking gets better as you get older** and higher in class, but it's still very expensive. If you park in an area without a permit, you'd swear a Parking Services person was in your back seat waiting for you to get out so they can ticket you!"

Q "I personally do not have a car on campus because **it would be more of a pain in the butt** than anything else. You have to pay a minimum amount for the year to park on-campus, and they specify which lot you get to park in. It may be considerably far from your living area."

Q "**Campus parking is a nightmare**. This year, it cost me a ton to park for the year, and I ended up really far from my building in a lot that wasn't completely paved and was prone to theft. I never had any problems with vandalism because I don't have a stereo system, but it wasn't uncommon to see cars in the Yellow Lot (underclassmen either park in yellow or purple lots) with broken windows and their stereos ripped out."

Q "The University tends to sell **more parking permits than there are spots**, so be prepared to spend a lot of time driving around looking for a place. As annoying as parking is on campus, having a car is a really nice convenience."

Q "Parking at UMass is a headache. And no matter how hard you try, your parking spot will always be the farthest point from the building you have to go to. **Don't bring a car here**—you don't need it, just make some friends who have cars."

The College Prowler Take On...
Parking

The quotes say it all; the parking situation at UMass is atrocious. The entire campus is surrounded by parking lots that are always packed and often unpaved. If you decide on bringing a car to UMass your freshman and sophomore years, do not bring a good one, or even one with a stereo. Having a car your junior and senior year if you live off campus makes more sense, but not much more. You will still have to walk great distances, drive around in circles looking for a spot, deal with bottomless potholes, and risk theft.

Something that people typically learn the hard way within weeks of arriving in Amherst is that meter maids hand out violations like candy on Halloween. You'd swear the "Big Dig" was being funded by the ceaseless efforts of Amherst and UMass civil servants. The point, I promise I have one, is that bringing a car to UMass as a freshmen and sophomore is more inconvenient than convenient. Besides, there isn't anywhere you'll need to go on campus, and probably off campus as well, that a free bus ride can't accommodate. If you absolutely require some mode of transportation I recommend, in order of convenience: a bicycle, skateboard, scooter, rollerblades, street luge, pogo stick, figure skates, unicycle, stilts, swimming flippers, and lastly a car—get the point?

The College Prowler™ Grade on

Parking: F

A high grade in this section indicates that parking is both available and affordable, and that parking enforcement isn't overly severe.

Transportation

The Lowdown On...
Transportation

Ways to Get Around:
On Campus:
UMass Transit Service (http://www.umass.edu/campus_services/transit)

The Five-College Van Service (413-545-2086)

Public Transportation:
Pioneer Valley Transit Authority (PVTA), (413) 781-7882; Pick up bus schedules from the Campus Center Information Desk or online at http://www.pvta.com

Taxi Cabs
Red Cab, (413) 253-3333

Car Rentals
Alamo, local: none; national: (800) 327-9633, www.alamo.com

Avis, local: none; national: (800) 831-2847, www.avis.com

Budget, local: none; national: (800) 527-0700, www.budget.com

Dollar, local: none; national: (800) 800-4000. www.dollar.com

Enterprise, local: (413) 259-1188; national: (800) 736-8222, www.enterprise.com

Hertz, local: (413) 732-0715; national: (800) 654-3131, www.hertz.com

Car Rentals (continued...)
National, local: (413) 586-1201; national: (800) 227-7368, www.nationalcar.com

Best Ways to Get Around Town:
PVTA
UMass Transit
Your friend's car
A pair of sneakers

Ways to Get Out of Town:
PVTA
Five-College Van Service

Airlines Serving Hartford:
Air Canada Jazz, (800) 776-3000, www.aircanada.ca/

American Eagle, (800) 433-7300, www.americanair.com

Continental Express, (800) 525-0280, www.continental.com

United Express, (800) 748-8853, www.ual.com

US Airways Express, (800) 428-4322, www.usair.com

America West, (800) 235-9292, www.americawest.com

Delta, (800) 221-1212, www.delta.com

Northwest Airlines, (800) 225-2525, www.nwa.com

Airlines (continued...)
Southwest Airlines, (800) 435-9792, www.southwest.com

United Airlines, (800) 241-6522, www.ual.com

Skyway Airlines (800) 452-2022, www.midwestexpress.com

Airport:
Bradley International Airport in Hartford, Ct
(860) 292-2000
BDL is 44 miles away from UMass which translates to approximately 1 hour of driving time.

How to Get There:
Peter Pan Amherst Center Bus Terminal
79 South Pleasant Street
Amherst, Ma
(800) 343-9999

U-Mass Campus Center or Southwest Hampden Dining Common
(800) 343-9999
At U-Mass, tickets must be purchased in advance at Campus Center Office or the Southwest Hampden Dining Common. Buses stop in front of The Fine Arts Center at Haigis Mall.

Directions for Driving:

Route 9 West

I-91 South

Take Exit #40

Take CT-75 Exit towards Poquonock/Suffield

Turn right on Ella Grasso Turnpike

Follow signs

A Cab Ride to the Airport Costs: Too much, borrow a friend's car.

Amtrak:

The Amtrak Train Station is in Springfield, Ma, approximately 19 miles from campus. For schedule information, call (800) 872-7245. www.amtrak.com

Springfield Amtrak Train Station

66 Lyman Street

Springfield, Ma 01103

(413) 785-4230

Travel Agents:

Carroll Travel and Cruise Center

15 Cowles Lane

Amherst, Ma 01002

(413) 256-8931

Council Travel Service

44 Main Street

Amherst, Ma 01002

(413) 256-1261

Travel Loft

266 North Pleasant Street

Amherst, Ma 01002

(413) 256-6481

Travel Makers Inc.

321 Main Street

Amherst, Ma 01002

(413) 256-8228

Students Speak Out On...
Transportation

> "Public transportation is awesome! Pioneer Valley Transit Authority (PVTA) can take you to any of the five colleges in the area for free. Peter Pan buses can take you to New York City, Boston, and even Washington, DC. The system is very good and easy to use."

Q "**Most buses are free**—the only ones you need to pay for are Peter Pan buses, which cover long distances to other cities."

Q "There are buses that run all the time, **every day, to every place that you could ever think of!** There are northbound and southbound campus shuttles that stay on campus, and also multiple ones that go off-campus. You can always get a complete schedule for every route off the Internet, so you know when the bus will come."

Q "You can take buses pretty much anywhere, and **they're very convenient** for getting to any parties off campus. They always drop you off within walking distance."

Q "There is a bus that goes to the nearby mall about a half hour away. **You can get a bus to many of the apartment complexes** and the grocery store, too."

Q "**Transportation is great, and usually free**. There are already so many cars here, you might as well take the bus."

Q "**All the buses make big loops around town** so all you have to do is find a bus stop on the right side of the street. Even if you live off-campus you don't need a car here. The buses are packed in the mornings, and they pay students a lot of money to drive them, in case you were looking for a job."

Q "As far as getting to your classes is concerned, **you might as well take the bus**. If you need to go off campus though, it is nice to have a car. The traffic here is pretty brutal, especially right before the Coolie Dickinson Bridge in the afternoons. All in all I'd say that it's pretty easy to get where you need to go here."

Q "**PVTA, you can't go wrong**. They run late too, until 2 a.m. in the morning I think.'

The College Prowler Take On...
Transportation

The public transportation system at UMass and in Amherst virtually balances out the substandard parking situation. On campus, the bus stops are strategically located near classroom buildings, dormitories, libraries, and dining halls, and are frequented by a bus about every five to ten minutes. UMass shuttles are available for physically disabled persons and will go everywhere on campus. The best part is you don't even need a bus schedule because destinations are electronically displayed on the front and side of each bus. Taxi's are convenient if you need to get somewhere in the immediate area, that is, if you don't feel like walking.

Luckily, because so many students do bring their cars to school, the chances of you being able to catch a ride with someone else or borrow a friend's car are pretty good. In fact, the transportation here is so good that seeing a hitchhiker means you get to make a wish. Everything at UMass is only an arm's length away, unless there's traffic. An advantage of living in a fraternity or sorority is that you are equidistant from both campus and the center of town, both of which are within walking distance.

B

The College Prowler™ Grade on

Transportation: B

A high grade for Transportation indicates that campus buses, public buses, cabs, and rental cars are readily-available and affordable. Other determining factors include proximity to an airport and the necessity of transportation.

Weather

The Lowdown On...
Weather

Average Temperature
Fall: 49.60 °F
Winter: 25.00 °F
Spring: 46.00 °F
Summer: 68.66 °F

Average Precipitation
Fall: 3.98 in.
Winter: 3.41 in.
Spring: 3.84 in.
Summer: 3.95 in.

Students Speak Out On...
Weather

"Weather here is a bit crazy because it changes frequently. One minute it could be eighty degrees and next thing you know it's sixty degrees. When I say this, I am speaking in regards to spring and fall. Summers are hot, like everywhere else. Winters are really cold, and some years we get a lot of snow."

Q "It rains pretty often, especially in spring, but we've had mostly great weather the three years I've been here. Of course, **that's excluding the four feet of snow** we had my sophomore year."

Q "It's hot in the beginning of the fall semester and then cools toward the end. Conversely, it's cold at the beginning of the spring semester toward the end. We get a nice variety—**that's New England for you**. There isn't too much rain, but when there is, it's usually heavy downpours."

Q "New England has crazy weather. **It's very unpredictable**, but I love it! When it gets warm, just about everyone lays out on the 'Horseshoe', which is a place in Southwest."

Q "Ah, New England—the **weather changes more frequently than half the freshman guys' underwear!** People skipped class in the spring to lie out in the sun one year, then the next spring they were skipping class to avoid walking in the rain."

Q "Spring and summer are nice, and the **temperature doesn't get above ninety degrees**. Fall is incredibly beautiful out here, and winter is good, but only if you like snow."

Q "**Fall at UMass is arguably the finest in the country**. I've lived in New England all my life and I've found the western Massachusetts area to be particularly beautiful in the spring and fall."

Q "This year the weather has sucked so far, **a lot of snow and even more rain**. Autumn here is always nice, I wish it was autumn all year-round. The temperature here changes very often and quickly, we get some great thunder and lightening storms as well."

Q "I have never seen so much snow, and **why is it all yellow near the frat houses?** Who says frat guys can't spell their own names?"

Q "I have never been out of New England so I'll have to say that **the weather here is normal**. I wouldn't mind living somewhere warmer during the winter though."

The College Prowler Take On...
Weather

Meteorology in New England is similar to astrology; you'd do just as well predicting the weather by using tarot cards. None of the seasons are consistent with the previous year's, and each one is dramatically different. This is good news if you are an outdoors person because it means an endless supply of things to do. The average temperatures listed at the beginning of this section don't really do weather at UMass justice since everything is in a constant state of change. Some years you may get numerous feet of snow, and some years you may be playing soccer in November. This category really depends on what you are use to and what's important to you.

Unless you have a condition, weather should be the last criteria you consider when choosing a college. However, if weather is an important factor to you, realize that when you come here and hate the climate, it probably won't be like that in two to three weeks. During the winters that we get a lot of snow (like this year), a lot of the students grab trays from the dining Commons and go sledding at a large hill in the Central residence area. As expressed in the quotes, the fall here is something you will never forget. So, if you haven't yet experienced one; now is your chance, but don't forget warm clothes!

The College Prowler™ Grade on

Weather: C+

A high Weather grade designates that temperatures are mild and rarely reach extremes, that the campus tends to be sunny rather than rainy, and that weather is fairly consistent rather than unpredictable.

Report Card Summary

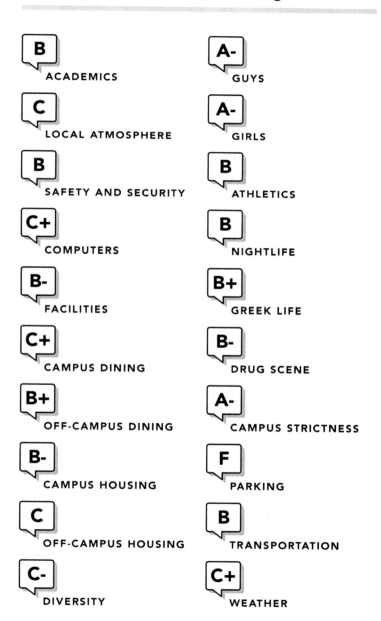

B ACADEMICS

A- GUYS

C LOCAL ATMOSPHERE

A- GIRLS

B SAFETY AND SECURITY

B ATHLETICS

C+ COMPUTERS

B NIGHTLIFE

B- FACILITIES

B+ GREEK LIFE

C+ CAMPUS DINING

B- DRUG SCENE

B+ OFF-CAMPUS DINING

A- CAMPUS STRICTNESS

B- CAMPUS HOUSING

F PARKING

C OFF-CAMPUS HOUSING

B TRANSPORTATION

C- DIVERSITY

C+ WEATHER

Overall Experience

Students Speak Out On...
Overall Experience

"It's a great place, with lots of opportunities. Despite some of the recent budget cuts, I am really happy here. I know that the university will get back on its feet and fix things up eventually, hopefully by reinstating escort services, supporting some of the smaller sports teams, and providing university child care."

"My overall experience with the school was a good one and it was a lot of fun. **I continued to meet new people** right through graduation. Everyday was an experience, and you can make it fun if you want to. I never wished I was somewhere else."

Q "At first, I didn't want to come here, but it kind of ended up being where I had to go. **Now I wouldn't go any where else**. There's so much to do and see—it's great."

Q "I love UMass. **The people are great**, and the classes and social life are a lot of fun. Sometimes it's tough to get into classes because of the huge number of people, which gets annoying, but you deal with it. I'm a Psychology major and I love it. The department is great! Our business program is amazing, too. I wouldn't want to be anywhere else. I'm a city girl, and it was tough to adapt to 'cow country'. Once you do, though, you really learn to appreciate the scenic area and the great people here."

Q "UMass really feels like home to me. **It's like living in a city** with so many people here, and I think it's more like real life because of the numbers. I still have a group of friends and I don't feel lost in the crowd at all. There are always events happening on campus, so you'll never get bored. The academics are also pretty good. Overall, it's a nice place to go to school."

Q "It's hard for me to say what my overall experience was at UMASS. **I absolutely loved it as a freshman**, but I was really sick the first semester last year, so I associate some bad things with being there. Just the same, I had a ton of fun and met a lot of amazing people. I am genuinely sad to leave. Right now things at UMass are a little uncertain because of budget cuts, but they're expected to be smoothed out within the next couple of years. In the mean time, getting into classes will probably be a huge pain. You should make sure the major you are interested in is not slated to be cut if the budget decreases continue."

Q "I've learned a lot about myself and other people out here. **It is a great place to simply do your thing** without many worries. The music and culture are great and the scenery is beautiful! I've spent three years out here so far, and even though it was a little difficult to adjust at first, I couldn't picture myself anywhere else."

Q "In the beginning, I didn't like it because I wasn't very outgoing, and you have to be at any big school. **It's easy to slip through the cracks** if you're not. My advice is to join clubs and other activities right away. I am on the ski team and I had the time of my life. I love UMass now and I definitely can't wait for next semester. There are so many good things that go on. My only concern is the budget cuts. You should definitely investigate, so you know if the major you want will still be here when you are."

Q "UMass is a great school. I definitely feel as though I got my money's worth. Like anything, **you get out of it what you put into it**. The people here are alright, and the teachers are really good. I went on exchange my junior year and had such a great time, and all for the same price you pay at UMass. I highly recommend that everyone exercise their option of going on exchange at some point. And if you do, look for a school that compliments UMass by providing things that UMass doesn't or can't. Over all I am glad that I went to school here, even though my parents couldn't find me at my graduation because there were so many people."

Q "I learned a lot here, about a lot of things. **What you learn at college doesn't all come from a text book**. It's funny because your senior year you think 'I can't wait to get out of here', but once you finally graduate you think 'What now? I wish I was still in school!'. It's a mixed bag really, but overall I am glad that I went to UMass, I will leave with many good memories."

The College Prowler Take On...
Overall Experience

My overall experience at UMass was a very positive one. Those of you who have now read this book and are going to attend UMass are lucky because the things which took me a few years to improve upon and figure out, you now know. I wish a lot of things were handled differently at UMass, and I know that I speak for a lot of people when I say that one of those things is the budget cuts. Yet, UMass's financial situation will improve over time, and may never even affect you. Coming to UMass has truly enriched my life with everything I have learned, and all the people I have met.

Despite the bad parking, unpredictable weather, and crumby campus dining, I've never been told by someone that they genuinely hate UMass, and likewise, I've never felt that way. If you work hard and don't let yourself get too distracted by all the parties, you will be able to avoid some of the pitfalls plaguing students fresh out of high school who aren't used to such responsibility. Going to UMass and experiencing such a multifaceted institution will open doors for you. The size of UMass was never a problem for me, if anything, it provided me with more resources and options. So do what I did, have fun.

The Inside Scoop

The Lowdown On...
The Inside Scoop

UMass Slang:

Know the slang, know the school. The following is a list of things you really need to know before coming to UMass. The more of these words you know, the better off you'll be.

The DC: Dining Common (cafeteria)

Puffer's: Puffer's Pond, a popular swimming hole near campus

The Bowl: Orchard Hill area where people congregate

The Quad: Campus Pond or the Northeast Quad

Haigis Mall: Area in front of the Fine Arts Center, not really a mall

Round Robin: A drinking event that occurs in the dorms

Rape Trails: Various trails around campus through secluded spots that students sometimes take as short cuts, at their own risk.

Whitless/Shitmore: The Whitmore Administration building

Frat Row: The Street between campus and Amherst center where most of the frats are located

Grinder: A submarine sandwich/hoagie

The Horseshoe: A wrap-around road in Southwest near the basketball courts

→

The Fart Center: Fine Arts Center

Shotgun: A method of chugging a beer straight from the can. The tab gets cracked slightly and a large hole to drink from is cut in the side of the can.

The Cage: Curry Hicks Athletic Field

The Zoo: UMass

The Cluster Office: Every three dorms or so have a "headquarters" where students can obtain different objects or services. This is also where students have to report when they get in trouble.

Cluster F@#ked: A student who has to report to the cluster office because they got caught doing something.

Wicked: Very

Things I Wish I Knew Before Coming to UMass

- Lost or stolen dorm room keys cost $160 dollars to replace.

- If you are unable to register for a course online or via telephone, you can still approach the professor and ask him/her
to be admitted.

- Fake ID's do not work well here.

- Buying anything but the most basic/inexpensive meal plan is a complete waste of money.

- How to manage my time better.

- Instead of buying your textbooks at the Textbook Annex, it makes more sense to either split the cost with someone else in the class, buy the books online (amazon.com), or see if the library has what you need.

- Just because you need a course doesn't mean you will get it.

- Going on exchange for a semester or two is comparable in cost to attending UMass for that same amount of time.

- Don't skip orientation.

- One bad grade can really bring down your cumulative GPA. And averages are hard to recover

Tips to Succeed at UMass

- Go to class, sounds like common sense but still very important

- Work hard and play hard, balance these things in your life

- Take every extra credit opportunity you can, don't be lazy

- Keep an assignment book, write down and mark off all of your assignments

- Do an internship

- Try to develop a schedule for studying

UMass Urban Legends

Every year, the rumor that Bill Cosby is going to speak at graduation gets circulated around the entire campus

If your roommate commits suicide, you will be granted straight A's for that semester

School Spirit

The school spirit at UMass is not what it used to be, partially because the athletic department has been downsized over the last couple years. However, certain sporting events are still a big draw at UMass like Midnight Madness and the Home Coming football game.

Traditions

Streaking

Fall and spring streaking happens each semester before finals. Maybe as a way to blow off steam, hundreds of UMass students will run but naked through the Northeast Quad at night as a break from studying.

Finding a Job or Internship

The Lowdown On...
Finding a Job or Internship

Many students who graduated in the spring of 2003 had trouble finding jobs. The economy is bad right now so not only were companies not hiring, but they weren't offering very exciting positions. Students can search for jobs and post their resumes with the Campus Career Network, although, limiting yourself to only one job source is not advisable during times like these.

Advice

It is my Belief that your ability to get a job after graduation relies heavily on how much experience you have. For this reason, I suggest that at some point during your four years at UMass, or however long it takes you to graduate, find and complete an internship that has some correlation with what you plan on doing after school. Also, make connections and do some serious networking, it's all about who you know and what you know.

Career Center Resources & Services

http://www-ccn.acad.umass.edu/index.htm

- Internships and Co-ops

- Cover letter, resume building and other career workshops

- Several career fairs

- Company directories and research

- Online resource for global newspapers and journals

- Career assistance by school or college

- Graduate school advising

- Student employment (work study financial aid)

- Advising and support services for students

Grads Who Enter Job Market within 6 Months of Graduation:
27%

Firms That Frequently Hire Graduates:
Price Waterhouse Coopers
Baystate Medical Center.

Alumni

The Lowdown On...
Alumni

Website:
http://www.umass.edu/
umhome/alumni/index.html, or
http://www.umassalumnionline
services.com

Office:
University of Massachusetts
Amherst Alumni Association

134 Hicks Way

Memorial Hall

Amherst, MA 01003-5410

Voice: (800) 456-UMASS or
(413) 545-2317

Fax: (413) 545-9433

E-Mail: alumni@admin.umass.
edu

Services Available
Career mentoring

Alumni career services

Business card exchange

Lifetime UMass email

Bulletin Boards

Class notes

Scholarships, grants, and
awards

Travel study program

Major Alumni Events

The biggest alumni events are; Reunions, Homecoming, and Regional Club Events in addition to special events. These include the Annual Salute to UMass Basketball, Distinguished Alumni Awards, and the occasional member only events.

Alumni Publications

• Massachusetts Review

• Alumni Gazette.

The Massachusetts Review comes out three times a year for alumni, students, and friends of the university, and is put out by Public Relations. The Alumni Gazette is part of the Massachusetts Review dedicated to alumni.

Did You Know?
Famous UMass Alumni:

Taj Mahal	Paul Theroux
Jack Welch	William Manchester
Julius Erving	Robert Meers
Jeff Corwin	George "Trigger" Burke
Norm Abram	Cynthia PerryBill Pullman
Briana Scurry	Carl Allen
Edwin Thomas	Kenneth Feinberg
Joseph Taylor	Michael Vespoli
Jack Canfield	Stephen Gluckstern
Bruce MacCombie	Hebert Bix
Frank Guidara	

Student Organizations

Active Ingredients- http://www.umass.edu/campact/active.html

Adventist Christians- http://www.umass.edu/campact/acts.html

African Student Association- http://www.umass.edu/rso/african/

Afrik-Am- http://www.umass.edu/campact/afrikam.html

AHORA- http://www.umass.edu/campact/ahora.html

ALANA Honor's Society- http://www.umass.edu/rso/alanaihs/

ALANA Nursing Association- http://www.umass.edu/campact/ana.html

Alchemists Anonymous- http://www.umass.edu/campact/alchem.html

Alive With Dance- http://www.umass.edu/campact/alivedan.html

Alliance Christian Fellowship- http://www.umass.edu/campact/alliance.html

Alpha Chi Omega- http://www.geocities.com/alphachideltamu/

Alpha Delta Phi- http://www.adphi.org/

Alpha Epsilon Phi- http://aephi.org/

Alpha Epsilon Pi- http://www.umass.edu/rso/aepi/

Alpha Kappa Alpha- http://www.umass.edu/greek/

Alpha Lambda Delta- http://www.umass.edu/campact/ald.html

Alpha Phi Alpha- http://www.umass.edu/greek/

Alpha Phi Omega- http://www-unix.oit.umass.edu/~aphio/

Alpha Tau Gamma- http://www.umass.edu/greek/

Amnesty International- http://www.umass.edu/rso/amnesty/

Ananda Marga Yoga Club- http://www.umass.edu/campact/ananda.html

Arab Students Association- http://www-unix.oit.umass.edu/~arab/

Art History Club- http://www.umass.edu/campact/art.html

Asian American Student Association- http://www-unix.oit.umass.edu/~aasa/

Baha'I Club- http://www.umass.edu/campact/bahai.html

Ballroom Dancing Club- http://www.umass.edu/rso/ballroom/

Bicycle Co-op- http://www.umass.edu/rso/bikecoop/

Bicycle Racing Club- http://www.umbrc.com/

Black Mass Communication Project- http://www.umass.edu/campact/bmcp.html

Black Student Union- http://www.umass.edu/campact/bsu.html

Boltwood Project- http://www.umass.edu/campact/boltwood.html

Boricuas Unidos- http://www.umass.edu/campact/boricuas.html

Boundaries: outlet of expression- http://www.umass.edu/campact/bound.html

Brothers and Sisters in Christ- http://www.umass.edu/campact/basic.html

Cambodian Student Association- http://www.umass.edu/campact/cambodia.html

Campus Center/Student Union Commission- http://www.aux.umass.edu/ccsucommission

Campus Crusade For Christ- http://home.ccci.org/umass/

Campus Design and Copy- http://www.umass.edu/cdcopy/

Campus Greens/Green Party- http://www.umass.edu/campact/cgreens.html

Cannabis Reform Coalition (CRC)- http://www-unix.oit.umass.edu/~cannabis/

Cape Verdean Student Alliance (CVSA)- http://www.umass.edu/rso/capeverd/

Capstone- http://www.umass.edu/campact/cso.html

Casa Dominicana (CASA)- http://www.umass.edu/campact/cso.html

Center for Student Businesses (CSB)- http://www.umass.edu/rso/csb/

Central Area Government- http://www.umass.edu/campact/cntrlgov.html

Chabad Students- http://www.umass.edu/campact/chabad.html

Chamber Choir- http://www.umass.edu/campact/chamber.html

Chess Club- http://www-ims.oit.umass.edu/chess/chess1.shtml

Chi Omega- http://www.umass.edu/greek/

Circle K Club- http://www.kiwanis.org/

The Massachusetts Daily Collegian- http://www.dailycollegian.com/

Comic Art Society- http://www.umass.edu/campact/comic.html

Commuter Area Government- http://www.umass.edu/campact/comtrgov.html

Commuter Services and Housing Resource Center- http://www-ims.oit.umass.edu/~cshrc

Concepto Latino- http://www.umass.edu/rso/concepto/

Craft Center- http://www.umass.edu/rso/craftctr/

Crew Club- http://www.umasscrew.com/home.asp

Dance Team- http://www.umass.edu/campact/dance.html

Debate Team- http://www.debate.vze.com/

Delta Sigma Theta- http://www.umass.edu/rso/deltasig/

Delta Upsilon- http://www.umass.edu/rso/deltau/

Delta Xi Phi- http://www.umass.edu/greek/

Delta Zeta- http://www.umass.edu/greek/

Distinguished Visitors Program- http://www.umass.edu/rso/dvp/

Earthfoods- http://www.umass.edu/rso/earthfds/

EMS- http://www.umass.edu/ems/

Environmental Horticulture Club- http://www-unix.oit.umass.edu/~envhort/HortClub/

English Speaking Caribbean Association- http://www.umass.edu/campact/esca.html

Eta Sigma Delta- http://www.umass.edu/campact/etasigd.html

Fencing Team- http://www.umass.edu/rso/fencing/

Figure Skating Club- http://www.umass.edu/rso/umfsc/

Flava Unit- http://www.umass.edu/campact/flava.html

Funk Team- http://www.umass.edu/campact/funk.html

Game Hobbyists League- http://www.umass.edu/rso/gameclub/

Gaming Club- http://www.umass.edu/campact/gaming.html

Gamma Phi Sigma- http://www.umass.edu/greek/

GardenShare- http://www.umass.edu/campact/garden.html

Golden Key Honor Society- http://www.umass.edu/campact/golden.html

Greek Affairs- http://www.umass.edu/greek/

Groove Phi Groove- http://www.umass.edu/greek/

Haitian American Students Association- http://www.umass.edu/rso/hasa/

Hang Gliding Club- http://www.umass.edu/rso/glide/

Hotel Managers- http://www.umass.edu/rso/uhm/

Index (Yearbook)- http://www.umass.edu/rso/index/

Institute of Industrial Engineers- http://www.ecs.umass.edu/iie/

Interfraternity Council- http://www.umass.edu/greek/ifc/

International Relations Club- http://www-unix.oit.umass.edu/~irclub/

International Socialist Organization- http://www.umass.edu/campact/iso.html

Intervarsity Christian Fellowship- http://www.umass.edu/rso/ivcf/

Investment Club- http://www.umass.edu/campact/invest.html

Iota Gamma Upsilon- http://www.iotagammaupsilon.com/

Iota Phi Theta- http://www.umass.edu/greek/

Japan America Club- http://www.umass.edu/rso/japanam/

Japanese Animation and Mange Society- http://www.umass.edu/rso/umjams/

Jewish Student Union- http://www-unix.oit.umass.edu/~jsu/

Juggling Club- http://www.umass.edu/rso/juggle/

Kappa Alpha Psi- http://www.umass.edu/greek/

Kappa Kappa Gamma- http://www.umass.edu/greek/

Kappa Kappa Psi/Tau Beta Sigma- http://www.umass.edu/band/kkpsi/

Kappa Phi Lambda- http://www.umass.edu/greek/

Kendo Club- http://www.umass.edu/campact/kendo.html

Korean Student Association- http://www.umass.edu/campact/ksa.html

Lambda Phi Epsilon- http://umasslambdas.com/

Lambda Pi Chi- http://www.geocities.com/lpciota/

Lambda Upsilon Lambda- http://www.launidadlatina.org/

Macintosh Users Group- http://www.umass.edu/campact/mac.html

MASSPIRG- http://www.umass.edu/rso/masspirg/

Medieval Swordsmanship Club- http://www.umass.edu/rso/swords/

Men's Lacrosse- http://www.umass.edu/rso/clublax/

Mercy House- http://www.umass.edu/campact/mercy.html

Motorsports Club- http://www.geocities.com/motorcity/factory/5408

Muslim Student's Association- http://www-unix.oit.umass.edu/~muslim/

National Pan-Hellenic Council- http://www.umass.edu/greek/nphc/index.html

National Society For Black Engineers- http://www.ecs.umass.edu/nsbe/

National Student Exchange Club- http://www.umass.edu/campact/natexch.html

Native American Student Association- http://www.umass.edu/campact/nasa.html

National Society of Collegiate Scholars- http://www.umass.edu/campact/nscs.html

Navigators- http://www-unix.oit.umass.edu/~navs/

Newman Student's Association- http://www.umass.edu/catholic/

Northeast Are Government- http://www.umass.edu/rso/neag/

NSSLHA- http://www.umass.edu/rso/nsslha/

Office of ALANA Affairs- http://www.umass.edu/alana/

Omega Delta- http://www.umass.edu/greek/

Orchard Hill Area Government- http://www.umass.edu/rso/ohag/

Outing Club- http://www-unix.oit.umass.edu/~outing/

Paintball Club- http://www.umass.edu/rso/paintball/

Panhellenic Council- http://www.umass.edu/rso/paintball/

People's Market- http://www.peoplesmarket.org/

Persian Student Organization- http://www.umass.edu/rso/persian/

Phi Beta Sigma- http://www.umass.edu/greek/

Phi Sigma Kappa- http://www.phisigmakappa.org/

Phi Sigma Pi- http://www.umass.edu/campact/phisigpi.html

Philosophical Society- http://www.umass.edu/campact/philo.html

Society of Physics Students- http://www.umass.edu/campact/physics.html

Pi Delta Psi- http://www.umasspdpsi.com/

Pi Lambda Phi- http://www.umass.edu/greek/ifc/

Pi Sigma Alpha- http://www.umass.edu/campact/pisiga.html

Polo Club- http://www.umass.edu/campact/polo.html

Pre-Vet & Animal Science Club- http://www.geocities.com/umassansciclub/

Pride Alliance- http://www.umass.edu/rso/pride/

Radical Student Union- http://www.umass.edu/rso/rsu/

Republican Club- http://www.umass.edu/rso/republcn/

Rugby Club- http://www.ecs.umass.edu/rugby/

Russian Student Organization- http://www.umass.edu/campact/russian.html

Sailing Team- http://www.umass.edu/rso/sailing/

S.C.E.R.A.- http://www.umass.edu/rso/scera/

Science Fiction Conventioners of UMass- http://www.umass.edu/rso/scum/

Science Fiction Society- http://www.umass.edu/rso/scifi/

SHARE- http://www.umass.edu/rso/share/

Shortcuts- http://www.umass.edu/rso/shortcut/

Shotokan Club- http://www.umass.edu/rso/shotokan/

Sigma Alpha Lambda- http://www.umass.edu/campact/sal.html

Sigma Alpha Mu- http://www.umass.edu/greek/

Sigma Delta Tau- http://www.sigmadeltatau.com/

Sigma Gamma Rho- http://www.umass.edu/greek/

Sigma Kappa- http://www-unix.oit.umass.edu/~lbelding/sigmak-appa/

Sigma Lambda Upsilon- http://www.sigmalambdaupsilon.org/

Sigma Phi Epsilon- http://www.umass.edu/rso/sigep/

Sigma Psi Zeta- http://www.umass.edu/greek/

Sigma Tau Gamma- http://www.umass.edu/greek/ifc/stg.htm

Silent Majority- http://www.minuteman-newspaper.com/

Simulation Gaming Association - http://www.ursga.org/

Ski & Board Club- http://www.umass.edu/rso/skiclub/

Sky Diving Club- http://www.umass.edu/campact/skydiving.html

Smash Videogamers Club

Snowboarding and Skateboarding- http://www.umass.edu/cam-pact/ssuma.html

Society of Hispanic Professional Engineers- http://www.umass.edu/rso/shpe/

Society of Women Engineers- http://www.ecs.umass.edu/swe/

Soul TV- http://www.umass.edu/campact/soul.html

South Asian Student Association- http://www.umass.edu/rso/sasa/

Southwest Area Government- http://www.umass.edu/campact/swag.html

Sports Managers of Color- http://www.umass.edu/campact/sprtoclr.html

S.A.M.B.A.- http://www.umass.edu/rso/samba/

Student Pagans Integrating Religion and Life- http://www.umass.edu/rso/spirals/

Students Together in Networking Graduates (STING)

Stockbridge Senate- http://www.umass.edu/campact/stckbrdg.html

Student Alumni Relations- http://www.umass.edu/rso/stars/index.html

Student Film Society- http://www.umass.edu/campact/sfs.html

Students For a Free Tibet- http://www.umass.edu/rso/fretibet/index.html

Student Government Association- http://www.umass.edu/rso/sga/

Student Legal Services Office- http://www-saris.admin.umass.edu/slso/

Student Nurses Association- http://www.umass.edu/campact/sna.html

Student Society of Arboriculture- http://www.umass.edu/campact/arbor.html

Student Sports Managers- http://www.umass.edu/campact/umassm.html

Student Union Art Gallery- http://www.umass.edu/rso/artspace/

Student Valley Productions- http://www-unix.oit.umass.edu/~svp/

Sweets and More- http://www.umass.edu/campact/sweets.html

Sylvan Area Government- http://www.geocities.com/sylvanarea-government/

Sylvan Snack Bar- http://www.umass.edu/rso/sylvansn/

Tai Chi Club- http://www.umass.edu/campact/tai.html

Taiwanese Student Association- http://www.umass.edu/campact/tsa.html

Theatre Guild- http://www.umass.edu/rso/guild/

Theta Chi- http://www.umass.edu/greek/

Tickets Unlimited- http://www.umass.edu/campact/tix.html

Thelion Quizbowl Society- http://sa.Massachusetts.edu/thelion/

Undergraduate Council in Religion & Classics - http://www.Massachusetts.edu/college/REL/council.html

Undergraduate Council of Gender and Women's Studies

Undergraduate Economics Council - http://www.econ.Massachusetts.edu/economicscouncil/

Undergraduate Film & Media Studies Council

Undergraduate History Council - http://www.Massachusetts.edu/college/HIS/undergrad/activities.html

Undergraduate Musicians' Council

Undergraduate Neuroscience Council - http://www.bcs.Massachusetts.edu/council/

Undergraduate Political Science Council - http://www.Massachusetts.edu/college/PSC/undergrad/news.php

University Democrats- http://www.umass.edu/campact/udems.html

University Productions and Concerts- http://www.geocities.com/upcpromos/

Up Til Dawn – community service project

UVC-TV 19- http://www-unix.oit.umass.edu/~uvctv19/

Vietnamese Student Association- http://www-unix.oit.umass.edu/~vietnam/

Vocal Suspects- http://www.vocalsuspects.org/

Volleyball Club (men's)- http://www-unix.oit.umass.edu/~volleybl/

Water Polo Club (men's)- http://www.umass.edu/campact/water-polo.html

Water Polo Club (women's)- http://www.umass.edu/campact/wwater.html

Wazobia Group- http://www.umass.edu/campact/wazobia.html

Wildlife Society- http://www.umass.edu/rso/wildlife/

WMUA Radio Station- http://www.wmua.org/

Women In Sports Management- http://www.umass.edu/rso/wism/

Women's Ice Hockey- http://www-unix.oit.umass.edu/~womhocke/

Women's Rugby Team- http://www.ecs.umass.edu/rugby/

Women's Volleyball Club- http://www.umass.edu/campact/wvolley.html

Wrestling Club- http://www.umass.edu/campact/wrestling.html

Zoo Disc Frisbee Team- http://www.umass.edu/campact/zoo.html

Zeta Beta Tau- http://www-unix.oit.umass.edu/~zbtumass/

The Best & The Worst

The Ten **BEST** Things About UMass:

1	Parties
2	Great Teachers
3	Low Tuition
4	Variety Of Majors
5	Library
6	Career Services
7	Location
8	Student Resources
9	Quality of Education
10	Campus Pond

The Ten **WORST** Things About UMass:

1	Budget Cuts
2	Parking
3	Office of Information Technology
4	Expensive Textbooks
5	Campus Dining
6	How Far You Have to Walk to Get to Class
7	Ugly Buildings
8	Registering for Classes
9	Reputation
10	Dormitories

Visiting UMass

The Lowdown On...
Visiting UMass

Hotel Information

Allen House Victorian Bed and Breakfast
http://www.allenhouse.com/
599 Main St
Amherst, Ma
(413) 253-5000
Distance from Campus: walking
Price Range: $75-175

Amherst Motel
http://www.amherstarea.
com/business/index.cfm/fa/
showBusiness/CompanyID/
108.cfm
408 Northampton Rd
Amherst, Ma
(413) 256-8122
Distance from Campus:
2.65 miles

→

Black Walnut Inn

http://www.blackwalnutinn.com/

1184 North Pleasant St

Amherst, Ma

(413) 549-5649

Distance from Campus: 2.1 miles

Campus Center Hotel

http://www.aux.umass.edu/hotel/

1 Campus Center Way

Amherst, Ma

(413) 549-6000

Distance from Campus: 0

Lord Jeffery Inn

http://www.lordjefferyinn.com/

30 Boltwood Ave

Amherst, Ma

(413) 253-2576

Distance from Campus: 7 miles

Price Range: $89-209

Parsonage Bed and Breakfast

1170 North Pleasant St

Amherst, Ma

(413) 549-1466

Distance from Campus: 1.7 miles

Travel Loft

http://www.amherstarea.com/business/index.cfm/fa/showBusiness/CompanyID/463.cfm

266 North Pleasant St

Amherst, Ma

(413) 256-6481

Distance from Campus: 1 mile

University Motor Lodge

http://travel.yahoo.com/p/hotel/355819

345 North Pleasant St.

Amherst, Ma

(413) 256-8111

Distance from Campus: .5 miles

Price Range: $50-100

Take a Campus Virtual Tour

http://www.umass.edu/cvtour/

Schedule a Group Information Session or Interview

Visit the University Admissions Center and speak with a Student Admissions Representative about various aspects of college life. These interviewers are formally trained students and are an excellent source of information. Contact the Undergraduate Admissions Office at (413) 545-0222 to schedule an informal non-evaluative interview.

Admissions Information Sessions are typically held in the Lincoln Campus Center at 12:30 p.m. every day except Sundays, Christmas week, the University Thanksgiving Break, the University March Break, legal holidays, including Memorial Day weekend and Labor Day weekend, and weekends during the months of June, July, and August. Reservations are not needed. Check at the Robsham Memorial Visitor's Center for the exact location on the day of your visit.

Campus Tours:

Student-led walking tours provide an overview of academic programs and campus life. Tours last about seventy-five minutes and leave from the Campus Center Information Desk at 11 a.m. and 1:30 p.m. every day, except Christmas week, the University Thanksgiving Break, the University March Break, legal holidays, including Memorial Day weekend and Labor Day weekend, and weekends during the months of June and July. Please note that during summer months access to academic buildings is limited, since school is not in session. For more information, call Campus Tours at (413) 545-4237.

Directions to Campus

Driving from the North:
- I-91 South
- Exit 24
- Route 9 East

Driving from the South:
- I-91
- Exit 24
- Right onto Route 9 East

Driving from the East:
- I-90 West
- Exit 4
- I-91 North
- Exit 24
- Route 9 East

Driving from the West:
- I-90 East
- Exit 4
- I-91 North
- Exit 24
- Route 9 East

Words to Know

Academic Probation – A student can receive this if they fail to keep up with their school's academic minimums. Those who are unable to improve their grades after receiving this warning can possibly face dismissal.

Beer Pong / Beirut – A drinking game with numerous cups of beer arranged in a particular pattern on each side of a table. The goal is to get a ping pong ball into one of the opponent's cups by throwing the ball or hitting it with a paddle. If the ball lands in a cup, the opponent is required to drink the beer.

Bid – An invitation from a fraternity or sorority to pledge their specific house.

Blue-Light Phone – Brightly-colored phone posts with a blue light bulb on top. These phones exist for security purposes and are located at various outside locations around most campuses. If a student has an emergency or is feeling endangered, they can pick up one of these phones (free of charge) to connect with campus police or an escort service.

Campus Police – Policemen who are specifically assigned to a given institution. Campus police are not regular city officers; they are employed by the university in a full-time capacity.

Club Sports – A level of sports that falls somewhere between varsity and intramural. If a student is unable to commit to a varsity team but has a lot of passion for athletics, a club sport could be a better, less intense option. If a club sport still requires too much commitment, intramurals often involve no traveling and a lot less time.

Cocaine – An illegal drug. Also known as "coke" or "blow," cocaine often resembles a white crystalline or powdery substance. It is highly addictive and dangerous.

Common Application – An application that students can use to apply to multiple schools.

Course Registration – The time when a student selects what courses they would like for the upcoming quarter or semester. Prior to registration, it is best to have an idea of several back-up courses in case a particular class becomes full. If a course is full, a student can place themselves on the waitlist, although this still does not guarantee entry.

Division Athletics – Athletics range from Division I to Division III. Division IA is the most competitive, while Division III is considered to be the least competitive.

Dorm – Short for dormitory, a dorm is an on-campus housing facility. Dorms can provide a range of options from suite-style rooms to more communal options that include shared bathrooms. Most first-year students live in dorms. Some upperclassmen who wish to stay on campus also choose this option.

Early Action – A way to apply to a school and get an early acceptance response without a binding commitment. This is a system that is becoming less and less available.

Early Decision – An option that students should use only if they are positive that a place is their dream school. If a student applies to a school using the early decision option and is admitted, they are required and bound to attend that university. Admission rates are usually higher with early decision students because the school knows that a student is making them their first choice.

Ecstasy – An illegal drug. Also known as "E" or "X," ecstasy looks like a pill and most resembles an aspirin. Considered a party drug, ecstasy is very dangerous and can be deadly.

Ethernet – An extremely fast internet connection that is usually available in most university-owned residence halls. To use an Ethernet connection properly, a student will need a network card and cable for their computer.

Fake ID – A counterfeit identification card that contains false information. Most commonly, students get fake IDs and change their birthdates so that they appear to be older than 21 (of legal drinking age). Even though it is illegal, many college students have fake IDs in hopes of purchasing alcohol or getting into bars.

Frosh – Slang for "freshmen."

Hazing – Initiation rituals that must be completed for membership into some fraternities or sororities. Numerous universities have outlawed hazing due to its degrading or dangerous requirements.

Sports (IMs) – A popular, and usually free, student activity where students create teams and compete against other groups for fun. These sports vary in competitiveness and can include a range of activities—everything from billiards to water polo. IM sports are a great way to meet people with similar interests.

Keg – Officially called a half barrel, a keg contains roughly 200 12-ounce servings of beer and is often found at college parties.

LSD – An illegal drug. Also known as acid, this hallucinogenic drug most commonly resembles a tab of paper.

Marijuana – An illegal drug. Also known as weed or pot; besides alcohol, marijuana is one of the most commonly-found drugs on campuses across the country.

Major –The focal point of a student's college studies; a specific topic that is studied for a degree. Examples of majors include physics, English, history, computer science, economics, business, and music. Many students decide on a specific major before arriving on campus, while others are simply "undecided" and figure it out later. Those who are extremely interested in two areas can also choose to double major.

Meal Block – The equivalent of one meal. Students on a "meal plan" usually receive a fixed number of meals per week.

Each meal, or "block," can be redeemed at the school's dining facilities in place of cash. More often than not, if a student fails to use their weekly allotment of meal blocks, they will be forfeited.

Minor – An additional focal point in a student's education. Often serving as a compliment or addition to a student's main area of focus, a minor has fewer requirements and prerequisites to fulfill than a major. Minors are not required for graduation from most schools; however some students who want to further explore many different interests choose to have both a major and a minor.

Mushrooms – An illegal drug. Also known as "shrooms," this drug looks like regular mushrooms but are extremely hallucinogenic.

Off-Campus Housing – Housing from a particular landlord or rental group that is not affiliated with the university. Depending on the college, off-campus housing can range from extremely popular to non-existent. Those students who choose to live off campus are typically given more freedom, but they also have to deal with things such as possible subletting scenarios, furniture, and bills. In addition to these factors, rental prices and distance often affect a student's decision to move off campus.

Office Hours – Time that teachers set aside for students who have questions about the coursework. Office hours are a good place for students to go over any problems and to show interest in the subject material.

Pledging – The time after a student has gone through rush, received a bid, and has chosen a particular fraternity or sorority they would like to join. Pledging usually lasts anywhere from one to two semesters. Once the pledging period is complete and a particular student has done everything that is required to become a member, they are considered a brother or sister. If a fraternity or a sorority would decide to "haze" a group of students, these initiation rituals would take place during the pledging period.

Private Institution – A school that does not use taxpayers dollars to help subsidize education costs. Private schools typically cost more than public schools and are usually smaller.

Prof – Slang for "professor."

Public Institution – A school that uses taxpayers dollars to help subsidize education costs. Public schools are often a good value for in-state residents and tend to be larger than most private colleges.

Quarter System (sometimes referred to as the Trimester System) – A type of academic calendar system. In this setup, students take classes for three academic periods. The first quarter usually starts in late September or early October and concludes right before Christmas. The second quarter usually starts around early to mid–January and finishes up around March or April. The last quarter, or "third quarter," usually starts in late March or early April and finishes up in late May or Mid-June. The fourth quarter is summer. The major difference between the quarter system and semester system is that students take more courses but with less coverage.

RA (Resident Assistant) – A student leader who is assigned to a particular floor in a dormitory in order to help to the other students who live there. A RA's duties include ensuring student safety and providing guidance or assistance wherever possible.

Recitation – An extension of a specific course; a "review" session of sorts. Because some classes are so large, recitations offer a setting with fewer students where students can ask questions and get help from professors or TAs in a more personalized environment. As a result, it is common for most large lecture classes to be supplemented with recitations.

Rolling Admissions – A form of admissions. Most commonly found at public institutions, schools with this type of policy continue to accept students throughout the year until their class sizes are met. For example, some schools begin accepting students as early as December and will continue to do so until April or May.

Room and Board – This is typically the combined cost of a university-owned room and a meal plan.

Room Draw/Housing Lottery – A common way to pick on-campus room assignments for the following year. If a student decides to remain in university-owned housing, they are assigned a unique number that, along with seniority, is used to choose their new rooms for the next year.

Rush – The period in which students can meet the brothers and sisters of a particular chapter and find out if a given fraternity or sorority is right for them. Rushing a fraternity or a sorority is not a requirement at any school. The goal of rush is to give students who are serious about pledging a feel for what to expect.

Semester System – The most common type of academic calendar system at college campuses. This setup typically includes two semesters in a given school year. The "fall" semester starts around the end of August or early September and finishes right before winter vacation. The "spring" semester usually starts in mid-January and ends around late April or May.

Student Center/Rec Center/Student Union – A common area on campus that often contains study areas, recreation facilities, and eateries. This building is often a good place to meet up with fellow students and is most commonly used as a hangout. Depending on the school, the student center can have a huge role or a non-existent role in campus life.

Student ID – A university-issued photo ID that serves as a student's key to many different functions within an institution. Some schools require students to show these cards in order to get into dorms, libraries, cafeterias, and other facilities. In addition to storing meal plan information, in some cases, a student ID can actually work as a debit card and allow students to purchase things from bookstores or local shops.

Suite – A type of dorm room. Unlike other places that have communal bathrooms that are shared by the entire floor, a suite has a private bathroom. Suite-style dorm rooms can house anywhere from two to ten students.

TA (Teacher's Assistant) – An undergraduate or grad student who helps in some manner with a specific course. In some cases, a TA will teach a class, assist a professor, grade assignments, or conduct office hours.

Undergraduate – A student who is in the process of studying for their Bachelor (college) degree.

ABOUT THE AUTHOR:

I graduated from UMass two months ago and writing this book was the first job I've found. I am originally from western Massachusetts so going to UMass seemed like the next logical step in my life after high school. I spent my entire junior year of college at the University of Alaska, Southeast in Juneau on a domestic exchange program. Although my degree is in Business Management, I have been interested in a career in writing for as long as I can remember.

I hope this book has been a useful resource for you. I approached this guidebook as objectively as possible, but of course every word I wrote will reflect the fact that my experiences at UMass have been uniquely personal. Many people in my life have been in some way responsible for the quality of this book, leaving myself the only one to blame for any mistakes and shortcomings, so instead of a list I would like to say thank you all. If anyone has any questions for me, about anything, email me at

"This isn't who it would be, if it wasn't who it is"

-Phish

Seth Pouliot

sethpouliot@collegeprowler.com

Notes

....
....
....
....
....
....
....
....
....
....
....
....
....
....

Notes

....

....

....

....

....

....

....

....

....

....

....

....

....

Notes

Notes

....

....

....

....

....

....

....

....

....

....

....

....

....

....

Notes

....

....

....

....

....

....

....

....

....

....

....

....

....

Notes

....

....

....

....

....

....

....

....

....

....

....

....

....

Notes

....

....

....

....

....

....

....

....

....

....

....

....

....

....

Notes

....

....

....

....

....

....

....

....

....

....

....

....

....

Notes

....

....

....

....

....

....

....

....

....

....

....

....

....

Notes

Notes

Notes

....

....

....

....

....

....

....

....

....

....

....

....

....

Notes

Need More Help?

Do you have more questions about this school? Can't find a certain statistic? College Prowler is here to help. We are the best source of college information on the planet. We have a network of thousands of students who can get the latest information on any school to you ASAP. E-mail us at *info@collegeprowler.com* with your college-related questions. It's like having an older sibling show you the ropes!

Email Us Your College-Related Questions!

Check out **www.collegeprowler.com** for more details.
1.800.290.2682

Notes

....

....

....

....

....

....

....

....

....

....

....

....

....

....

Tell Us What Life Is Really Like At Your School!

Have you ever wanted to let people know what your school is really like? Now's your chance to help millions of high school students choose the right school.

Let your voice be heard and win cash and prizes!

Check out **www.collegeprowler.com** for more info!

Notes

....

....

....

....

....

....

....

....

....

....

....

....

....

Do You Have What It Takes To Get Admitted?

The College Prowler Road to College Counseling Program is here. An admissions officer will review your candidacy at the school of your choice and create a 12+ page personal admission plan. We rate your credentials with the same criteria used by school admissions committees. We assess your strengths and weaknesses and create a plan of action that makes a difference.

Check out **www.collegeprowler.com** or call 1.800.290.2682 for complete details.

Notes

....

....

....

....

....

....

....

....

....

....

....

....

....

Pros and Cons

Still can't figure out if this is the right school for you?
You've already read through this in-depth guide; why not
list the pros and cons? It will really help with narrowing down
your decision and determining whether or not
this school is right for you.

Pros	Cons

Notes

....

....

....

....

....

....

....

....

....

....

....

....

....

Notes

Notes

Notes

....

....

....

....

....

....

....

....

....

....

....

....

....

Reach A Market Of Over 24 Million People.

Advertising with College Prowler will provide you with an environment in which your message will be read and respected. Place your message in a College Prowler guidebook, and let us start bringing long-lasting customers to you. We deliver high-quality ads in color or black-and-white throughout our guidebooks.

Contact Joey Rahimi
joey@collegeprowler.com
412.697.1391
1.800.290.2682

Check out **www.collegeprowler.com** for more info.

Notes

Write For Us!
Get Published! Voice Your Opinion.

Writing a College Prowler guidebook is both fun and rewarding; our open-ended format allows your own creativity free reign. Our writers have been featured in national newspapers and have seen their names in bookstores across the country. Now is your chance to break into the publishing industry with one of the country's fastest-growing publishers!

Apply now at **www.collegeprowler.com**

Contact *editor@collegeprowler.com* or call 1.800.290.2682 for more details.

Notes

....

....

....

....

....

....

....

....

....

....

....

....

....